THE FINAL WARNING

THE FINAL WARNING
and A Defense Against Modernism

Paul A. Mihalik, Sr.
Lt. Colonel USAF (Ret.)

Queenship
PUBLISHING COMPANY
P. O Box 42028 Santa Barbara, CA 93140-2028
(800) 647-9882 • (805) 957-4893 • Fax: (805) 957-1631

Dedication

This book is dedicated to the Mother of God, Her Angels, and the priests of the Marian Movement of Priests, living and deceased.

Eternal Father, I offer You the most Precious Blood of Your Divine Son, in union with all the Masses offered this day throughout the world, for the Holy Souls in Purgatory, especially the deceased religious and priests.

© 1997 Queenship Publishing

Library of Congress #: 97-69915

Published by:
    Queenship Publishing
    P. O. Box 42028
    Santa Barbara, CA 93140-2028
    (800) 647-9882 • (805) 957-4893 • Fax: (805) 957-1631

Printed in the United States of America

ISBN: 1-57918-043-4

Contents

PART ONE

THE WARNING

and A Defense Against Modernism

CHAPTER ONE
The Purpose of This Book

Sunday, March 9th, 1997, was a milestone for the people of southern Arizona. To my knowledge it was the first time a public acknowledgement was made from the pulpit of a Catholic Church in southern Arizona that we must make a choice for God and His commandments or suffer serious consequences in the form of a great apostasy, earthquakes, bad weather, wars and other punishments. The words were NOT speaking of the end of the world but the end of an era. These are words of Jesus and His Mother. When was the last time you heard about Fatima in a Church?

The priest made it clear that we are being duly warned by messages from Heaven. God bless the priest for his love of his people — enough to have the courage to believe and to warn his flock as its shepherd. It takes real courage nowadays for a priest to take this stance in view of the ridicule and scorn suffered when priests refer to Mary and Her messages.

God bless Fr. Antonio Ruiz of San Felipe de Jesus Church in Nogales, Arizona for his faith and courage to speak out for his people in this day of timid and intimidated Church leaders. His people are the beneficiaries of his courage and love of Mary and Her Church-approved message of Fatima.

This interim period in which we live is called the Tribulation which will be followed by a severe chastisement. These are not new and strange words to those members of the Church who have become familiar with the Church approved apparitions of La Salette and Fatima. The very sad fact is that the majority of Catholics know little or nothing of the warnings given to us at these two places and a good many other places since 1917 when Our Lady revealed the

1

Miracle of the Sun in Fatima, Portugal on Oct. 13. This phenomenon of the sun was witnessed by more than 70,000 people and reported in the newspapers of Portugal and other countries. Today it is known by relatively few.

Isn't it strange that although Pope John Paul II, the Vicar of Christ on earth, has attributed the saving of his life to Our Lady of Fatima there are some priests and Catholic lay persons who do not accept this event at Fatima as authentic? In spite of the predictions of Our Lady at Fatima concerning Russia and World War II, most Catholics seem unaware of those warnings which refer to consequences of the most frightening reality — those which might involve nuclear war and worldwide suffering.

Since 1973 the Blessed Virgin Mary has been allegedly speaking to an Italian priest who publishes these announcements in a book entitled *To The Priests, My Beloved Sons*. In Akita, Japan and Holland she has spoken in loving warnings to mankind to change and return to God. The responsible bishops of these places have approved these visits from heaven as worthy of our belief, as has also happened in Betania, Venezuela. In other places such as Medjugorje, Bosnia-Herzegovina, Garabandal, Spain, Dozule, France, Ireland, Africa and the United States, the Church is either investigating the serious warnings allegedly given to us through various visionaries or ignoring them for whatever reason.

All visions, apparitions, and locutions referenced in this book are either approved by the Church or under investigation. This aspect of current investigation carries a very important meaning and has critical bearing on the information contained in the messages herein offered. It required a period of some fourteen years before the Church approved the messages at Fatima as supernatural, while the world was not complying with Mary's request. The result? The record now shows that because the world did not comply with The Virgin's requests and warnings in sufficient time, the world suffered the effects of Communist atheism and World War II, the Korean War, the Vietnam War and other blood-letting disturbances coupled with a general loss of faith and a descent into depravity, murder, abortion, homosexuality, AIDS, and other new diseases. Famine has struck parts of the world. But few see the cause and effect!

2

The millions who visit Fatima, Lourdes, Akita, Betania and Medjugorje attest to the strong faith and belief in the messages from Mary who comes as a prophet of our times. Hundreds of books have been published by capable and believing authors, some of whom are priests of the Roman Catholic Faith. Yet millions have not even heard to this day of these messages and books which tell of the warnings of events to come in what might be the near future. Why have warnings not been made known in some systematic way for the benefit of the faithful and the masses at large?

The Church teaches that we are not *obligated* to believe private revelation but does it not concern us when the Vicar of Christ on earth believes in the message of Fatima and more than one Pope believes that the "smoke of Satan" has entered into the Church at the highest level?

This book is an attempt to tell in direct language the messages and warnings the Blessed Virgin Mary and Her Son are giving to mankind. (None of these messages teaches against the faith and morals taught by the Roman Catholic Church.) Some pilgrims on return from Fatima, Medjugorje, Betania, or Akita are so inspired as to embark on deep spiritual changes in their private lives. Many have taken on active roles in the Church to evangelize others and spread the good news of Jesus. Some have seen it as their obligation to make a public manifestation of their gratitude and love of God by extraordinary efforts and expense.

One such project in southern Arizona has done just that — The Cross Project of Our Lady of The Sierras Foundation. To many observers, especially those acquainted in detail of the efforts, humiliations, threats, and personal affronts in the press and in the courts of Arizona suffered by the members of this Foundation, there is no doubt that more than the hate and ignorance of some are at work. There has been such opposition to their plans to bring glory to the Cross of Jesus and His Mother that it appears a kind of diabolical hate has confronted their efforts. After three years of effort and ridicule, the Foundation has won through the courts, a building permit to erect a 32 ft statue of the Blessed Virgin Mary which directs the observer to a 70 ft. cross on the side of a beautiful mountain in the area of Sierra Vista, Arizona, south of Tucson.

The Foundation has donated one large cross to the Benedictine Monastery at St. David, Arizona. A member of the Foundation is now allegedly receiving locutions from Jesus and Mary.

In these times of the offending sights on television, in the movies, and publications, especially those against holy purity and chastity, the cross of our redemption and the image of the Mother of the Savior who draws us to Him, will be a magnificent sight against the natural beauty of God's creation, a beautiful mountain.

It is my hope that the reader will listen for the nudgings of the Holy Spirit to prepare for the extraordinary events coming soon according to Our Blessed Mother. The WARNING is one of our main concerns. Mary tells us we will "soon" have an experience from the Holy Spirit in which we will see the condition of our souls as God Himself sees us. She says we are receiving this gift of mercy which enables us to see the reality of our spiritual lives — good and bad — and we are given this opportunity to return to God and His commandments, or lose our souls for an eternity of hell without God. Thus the name of this book. Another kind of warning is presented here as well, and that is for all of us to be alert to erroneous teachings from the pulpit and in publications by those who have deserted the Catholic Faith but still call themselves Catholic while doing untold harm through the heresy of Modernism and New Age hocus-pocus. We should be grateful to Mary, Mother of God, Who is sent by Her Son to bring us warnings as a prophet of the end times. Lord, grant that all will be prepared for The Warning and its aftermath.

Thousands of good and holy priests are serving the Church. The critical words of Jesus and Mary quoted in the following messages are obviously *directed to those priests and bishops who are really no longer Roman Catholic in their faith, preaching, and conduct.* They remain in the Church to weaken and destroy it from within, "while heading for perdition and taking many of the faithful with them," according to Our Blessed Mother in Her recent messages. Heresies of all kinds are now gaining headway, especially the heresy of Modernism. Be alert. Filter through the teachings of the Magisterium all that you hear and read on spiritual matters. Use the official Roman Catholic Catechism. Do not take for granted that all parochial schools or universities are teaching the true Faith. Do not give your financial support to any parish or institution that preaches against the authentic teachings and traditions of the Catholic Church. Use your catechism and verify. The strongest attacks are against the divinity of Christ, the Real Presence in the Eucharist, the Resurrection of Jesus, and all things supernatural. This is the heresy of Modernism. It is your Church. Guard It! You have one soul. Protect it!

Paul A. Mihalik, Sr.
Patagonia, Arizona

March 19, 1997
Feast of St. Joseph, Patron of The Roman Catholic Church

The Final Warning

CHAPTER TWO
The Messages and Our Responsibility

The Communion of Saints

The people who make up the Church make up the Mystical Body of Christ and He is its Head. The Church teaches that this body of believers has an inherent resonsibility to work towards their individual salvation AND to pray for the conversion of souls. This term *conversion* does not mean we are to draw persons from one faith to another but to evangelize for their change from *lost* souls to souls burning with love of God as seen in their daily lives — into *saved* souls.

In every message since La Salette in 1846 to the present day we are reminded that God's plan of salvation uses our prayers, fasting, penance and good will to mysteriously bring souls from the brink of hell to a new life in God. In this Communion of Saints we prove our love of neighbor and of God by our concern for their souls although those souls may currently be totally indifferent to their eternal destiny. Before we are able to perform this great work of charity there has to exist a most loving, forgiving and merciful God Who accepts our offering on behalf of those poor souls still living on this earth but dead in their souls. God accepts our redemptive suffering as we cooperate with His eternal plans for souls. He accepts our prayers for the salvation of others.

Can our minds grasp the enormity of such love and mercy? Only in FAITH can we say yes to this responsibility and opportunity to play a role in salvation. And to such a privilege! Although not many are consciously aware of this responsibility everyone who prays the Our Father prays for other souls — *Forgive us our trespasses as we forgive those who trespass against us and lead us not into temptation but deliver us from evil.* In the Rosary Mary asks us to add this prayer after every decade — *O My Jesus, forgive us our sins and save us from the fires of hell, lead all souls to heaven, especially those who are in most need of your mercy.* It was once thought that this referred to the souls in Purgatory but it is now believed this refers to the begging of mercy for those souls who might otherwise be lost forever.

There is no real question about the motive in the prayer because in Mary's explicit words in Fatima, Garabandal, Akita and other places of apparitions or locutions She makes it clear that millions of souls might be lost "because they have no one to pray for them." And to really emphasize this point it should be pointed out that Mary has voiced the warning that in the coming *chastisement* millions will be lost if we do not pray for them. We have a beautiful challenge as Christians to participate in God's plan of salvation which will eventually be to God's greater glory and ours. And it is the most frightening responsibility for which we will answer to God at our partiular judgement if we squander these times because of spiritual sloth, lack of faith, or obstinancy in our sin and hate and indifference.

The Catholic people who are familiar with the messages from La Salette, Fatima, Akita, Garabandal, Kibeho, Betania, Fr. Gobbi, and other sources, as well as the devotions of The Divine Mercy and Living in The Divine Will, will recognize messages and warnings from Our Blessed Mother in the following poem titled *The Warning.* This title refers to those messages in which Mary tells us a time is coming "soon" during which every person on this earth of every religion will receive the Holy Spirit Who will allow us to see our souls the way God sees us.

Following this experience we will be given a period of time during which we can change our behavior if such change is needed and return to living the Ten Commandments in our return to God. Otherwise those who do not take advantage of this merciful revelation will surely lose their soul in the coming world punishment of this modern Sodom and Gomorrah. If the reader desires to determine what sense of urgency applies to these warnings, consider that Mary told Fr. Gobbi in 1988 that all She predicted beginning with La Salette to the current times will come to fruition "within 10 years." In 1995 Mary told Fr. Gobbi that by the Golden Jubilee year of 2000 Her Immaculate Heart will have already triumphed! What do you suppose faces us in the three intervening years? Following the poem in the next chapter are various messages from Heaven which might help answer this question.

THE WARNING

I hope to offer you sufficient information with which to convince you, the reader, to prepare yourself for "THE WARNING" — that event which is predicted by the Blessed Mother to take place "very soon" when every person who has attained the age of reason, will see the condition of their soul as God sees the soul.

Another warning is also presented in this book in order to alert you to be aware of the renegade priests and bishops, religious, and laity who are determined to literally steal your Catholic Faith away from you, your family, and friends while pretending to be faith-filled Catholic shepherds and teachers who have your spiritual welfare at heart. These false prophets and Judases are deliberate or naive tools of Satan. You desperately need to know the facts. They deperately need your prayers for conversion. You need to defend yourself through prayer and the Sacraments. They need to be challenged whenever they teach against the authentic teachings of the Church, including the encyclicals of the Holy Father.

A schism within the Church has been predicted by the Blessed Mother. Each of us who thinks we are prepared to live the Faith and defend the Faith is now asked to go well beyond a passive resistance to the attacks on our Catholic heritage and the Holy Father. We are asked to actively evangelize and challenge all error that we find being taught from the pulpit, in the Catholic schools and CCD classes, in prayer groups, Church councils, Church committees, and possibly from the chancery office itself. We have been and are being warned from Heaven that TIME IS SHORT and millions of souls are at risk of being lost forever. As members of the Communion of Saints, we have a most serious obligation to preserve the Faith and to save souls. Saving souls is not just for the clergy. We must love our neighbor to the point that we would fear the loss of even one soul. (See Christina Gallagher, Chapter Seven)

American Roman Catholics must recognize that we cannot simply rely on the truth always being taught from the pulpit or in the Catholic press. It is critical that each of us read and listen with discernment and with the authority of Canon Law on our side refuse any errors or deviation from the teachings of Jesus Christ and His Magisterium. Those loyal Catholics will constitute the remnant Jesus spoke of in the Gospel. We are the Church. We must defend that Church. In doing so, we defend Jesus Christ Himself, but only if we defend the AUTHENTIC ROMAN CATHOLIC CHURCH. We can fortify ourselves for this task by studying and knowing the contents of the authentic Catholic Catechism. For the Catholic who is serious about preparing for The Warning, does he or she need to be told that frequent sacramental confession is a must?

CHAPTER THREE

The Warning

Dearest Virgin Mary, you have come to tell us
That we are Your children — and how much You love us —
That You are crying for us — but we do not listen
Nor do we trust Your message and the time is near!

In the village by the mountains where the giant cross is standing
Where the church of James is singing in praise of the Risen One
You gave to us the message, but seldom do we listen
We seem to never listen — and the time is near!

Up there in the mountains in the little village
You spoke your special message in the grove of pines.
You said to Sister Agnes in the convent by the seashore
We will soon have much to suffer if we don't change our ways.

You cried for all the nations — one hundred times plus one
To warn us of the future because of what we've done.
We no longer say we've sinned against the Father,
Forgive us please dear Father. We say NOTHING is a sin!

The sun shone in the sky and it danced for You, dear Mother,
To tell us for the Father, He sent His Son to die.
He sent His Son to suffer and if we still continue
To say there is no sin — there is no need for sorrow
There is no hell to burn us — there is no evil in us —

Then we will see the curtain descend to bring the darkness,

Take away His light and leave us to ourselves
In the dismal darkness without His grace to guide us,
Without His love to warm us. Without the Host to feed us.

He'll give us what we wanted, what we surely asked for.
We turned from His own Mother. We turned from God Himself!
He'll give us what we wanted. WHAT WE SURELY ASKED FOR.
He'll leave us to ourselves!

The little St. Therese had tried to tell her story —
She has sent her many roses with her *little way.*
Today the modern prophets repeat her simple message —
To love God and our neighbor — to live her *little way.*

They give the sweetest message — that He will still forgive us
If we approach His mercy — if we ask forgivesness.
They tell us how we hurt Him. We're asked to do our duty.
To change our hearts and actions into the *little way.*

Our Blessed Mother speaks to all Her children;
"When you refuse to notice the needs of all the hungry,
Cold and broken-hearted, you turn away from Him!
When you avoid the people who simply want to be loved —
Who want someone to listen — you turn away from Him!

They need to hear "I love you." They learn from your example
They know that My Son loves them by your warm embrace.
"Come, I now forgive you — let My arms surround you —
I have always loved you" is what your actions say.

"But first they need to know Him — and they'll get to know Him
From your loving actions and your warm concern
And from caring and your sharing what He has given to you —
All your gifts and talents, all of your possessions —
This is what you all should do."

Then help us, loving Savior, to listen to Your Mother
Who comes with words of sadness and with Her bloody tears —

To believe what She is saying — *that the cup is overflowing*
and the WARNING is very near!

Our Lady speaks with sadness to tell all Her dear children:
"Soon you will hear the thunder — feel the earth be shaken,
See the sign of Jesus in the darkened sky.
You'll see your sins before you from your early childhood —
All of your transgressions to the present day!"

How can we survive this, tell us, dearest Mother
If we still offend Him and we're not truly sorry?
Help us — teach us, Mother that our very souls
Cry out for forgiveness — cry out for salvation —
Cry out for His love.

"Remove your pride and blindness so you can say you're sorry.
Confess to His good shepherds and start out once again
To be His little children — cleansed with His forgiveness
And love Him like a Father — go sit upon His knee."

Then send the Holy Spirit — we remnant scream to Heaven.
Some of us still love Him. Some of us still care.
Let the Holy Spirit send His fire upon us —
To make us all awaken and seek His Sacred Heart.

That Heart all torn and bleeding from the world's great evil —
From our ruthless actions — killing in the womb!
That Heart that can awaken our love for our Redeemer
And to see what the Father offers from His Holy Mother
And the God-man Son!

Our Lady speaks to warn us and She sadly says:

"Every man and woman, child and adolescent
Of all the world's religions will be called upon to see
Through God's swift revelation how you sinned against Him,
Of what you are deserving — a hell eternally.

"How you sinned against Him — how you hurt each other
How the evil travels — round and round it travels
To bring world desolation — war and crime and hunger —
To crush the souls of children — to steal the lives of babies
The lives of MY dear babies, still in their mother's womb.

"And how the smaller nations forever in their worry
From adjacent bullies that threaten them with war —
War that is born in man's pure evil, avarice, and pride
Growing in their hatred, from the Devil's seed."

Jesus speaks:

"Never fear I tell you. I am always with you.
You need to trust My Mercy. You need to change your ways.
I have sent My Mother but most of you ignore Her.
Most do not believe it. They say it isn't Her.

"My shepherds who *should* know Her — who are Her special sons —
Too many speak out against Her and say She isn't here!
They say these aren't the *end times* — that God loves all His people.
They say that I won't punish because I love you as you are.

"That is true, My children, but you must also be repentant —
Tell Me that you love Me and that you really care!
Some of My priest sons know only of My Mercy —
They know not yet My justice — they know only of My love.

"So I beg you all to listen to My beloved Mother —
Hear what She is saying from Her bleeding Heart.
Listen to Her pleading — She is My Special Prophet.
She speaks the words of warning — She speaks them out for Me —
For the Son She gave Her life to —
the Son who brought Her heart-break —
The Son who brought Her anguish *before* He brought redemption
Through Her co-operation — and opened Heaven's gates.

"Hear Her words of pleading 'Get ready for the WARNING.'
Live My Ten Commandments and live the *little way.*
Because soon you will be seeing all your sins before you —
See your evil nature from your greed and envy
From your evil gossip — from your lustful conduct —
And your gross behavior with your dance with death.

"The death of My little babies — those I sent to help you —
To bring you Heaven's answers to your many cancers and your
many woes —
The death of those I sent you in answer to the prayers
Of good and holy people — the courageous victim souls!

"Who said to Me, Dear Father, have mercy on Your children,
Please listen to our prayers — accept our good intentions —
Accept our pain and sufferings which we offer up to You
On behalf of these Your people who never think of You.

"But from My deepest Mercy I will send My Spirit
To bring You recognition of your state of soul —
Of how your Father sees you — how I, your Savior, know you
And the reckless movements of your faithless hearts.

"In My love and Mercy I await your answer —
If you can change your actions and change your stoney hearts
From stone into My image — humble hearts and gentle
As My little children — come sit upon My knee.

"Or — cold and unrepenting — hating Me and others —
Refusing My intentions to love and set you free.
If that is your decision — to spurn My sweetest offerings —
My justice will speak loudly when I leave you to yourselves!

"So love Me, My dear People — take My sweetest offerings —
I've given you My Mother, My Spirit, and My life!
Your choice for Me and Heaven will bring you joy forever
And with My Saints and Mother you will live forever more."

(P. Mihalik)

The Final Warning

CHAPTER FOUR

Modernism — A Heresy

Before I introduce you to Fr. Drexel and the strong words Our Lord gave to him for this generation of priests and laity, it might be helpful to give you a simple outline of the horrors of Modernism. Pope Pius X eliminated, for all practical purposes, this insidious heresy from the Church in his time. At least the heresy was under some control. However, due to laxity and failure of the Vatican to properly assess the strength and conviction of the liberal element within the Church, the loyal and orthodox bishops and cardinals were overwhelmed at Vatican Council II. Thus the liberal bishops managed to obtain sufficiently broad guidelines within the documents to be able to return to their dioceses and insist on their own liberal interpretation of the Council's efforts.

This was the beginning of the demise of the seminaries as we once knew them in the United States. Orthodoxy was out the window with the bath-water when the fresh-air reforms of Pope John XXIII were invoked. And everyone was asleep except the liberals who steamrolled over the Church and introduced the many changes in the seminaries that no longer support the teachings of the Church. Modernism had now raised its ugly head at the very place it could best due its damage to the priesthood.

There is a word that scares the pants off many people in sensitive positions of responsibility. I learned the real meaning of the word in the United States Air Force. The word is: accountability. It applies to bank presidents, to sergeants, to school principals, to generals, and to PRIESTS and BISHOPS. Take a real hard look at the words of Jesus when he spoke to Fr. Drexel and to Conchita in the following pages. It seems to me His bottom line goes something like this (I think you'll agree when you read the Chapter on Fr. Drexel):

"Priests, you are accountable to Me. You accepted ordination through your own free will. You made vows to serve Me. Your life is to be CONSUMED as you immolate yourself at the altar of service to your flock; not in hours of television that take you away from the Divine Office; the social drinking round in the elite communities; excessive time on the golf-course; the energy consumed in trying to be recognized and honored and promoted; and for you who organize yourselves to persecute and ostracize My faithful sons who are the orthodox lovers and followers of My Beloved Mother, the one and Holy Trinity, and My beloved spouse the Church. You need to look at My sons who make up the Marian Movement of Priests and others like them. These are the ones who are intimately familiar with words like immolate, sacrifice, prayer, service to the marginalized, the fallen and the sick. These, universally, are the ones, who, even in retirement, consume themselves, sometimes even in the service of those priests who have deserted Me — spending hours that could otherwise be spent in rest richly deserved — by serving Mass and forgiving sins in My name — because they ARE IN LOVE WITH THEIR CREATOR and THE ONE HOLIEST PRIEST WHOM they serve until they die lonely in hospitals and nursing homes... burnt out from loyal service to their flock and to Me, but on the verge of entering My Kingdom where I Myself will make their sacrifice honored and recognized and respected for all eternity. This generation of loyal priests will be represented once again in My priesthood when the purification of the Church and the world is complete and the Immaculate Heart of My Mother triumphs!"

Accountability! Priests have said to me that they themselves desire to see members of the priesthood held accountable. It would be obviously better for bishops and priests to fulfill their obligations on this earth than to be held accountable in the next life. Which brings me to the amazing video-tape I viewed recently which is a MUST

SEE bell-ringer! The name of the tape is *Prophecies and the New Times,* Max Kol productions. The priest has been a guest on Mother Angelica's television program. The video is about an experience Father Steven Scheier had after a head-on vehicle accident. Fr. Scheier found himself being judged by Jesus. He was condemned to HELL! Fr. Scheier says that all through the time during which Jesus is judging him, he, the priest, is agreeing with all of the accusations until finally Jesus says his sentence is to be in hell. At this point the priest hears a female voice but sees no one. The voice says to Jesus (I am paraphrasing) "Jesus, this is a son of mine. Please give him another chance." Jesus replies, "He is a priest and he served himself for his 12 years as a priest. He did not serve Me, but I will give him to You as you request." (I am still paraphrasing). This priest believes the Blessed Mother interceded for him and he was given his life again to change and save his soul. The priest goes on to say on the tape that he was too interested in raising funds and other activities that were not accomplishing much in the service of his flock and for Jesus. He worried about offending people with his homilies so he minced words and told them what they wanted to hear — NOT WHAT THEY NEEDED TO HEAR. For this he was condemned to hell!

Tough reading here for all of us. We are all going to be held accountable — priests, bishops, laity!

The Horrors of The Heresy of MODERNISM

Many bishops and priests have been drawn into the errors of this heresy. (Jesus says to Fr. Drexel this is the worst heresy). They were submerged in error in the seminaries and by the silent/secret members of Freemasonry who wear the Roman collar and who control many of our seminaries and many of the chanceries. These wayward priests and bishops were victimized by bishops who deliberately or through unholy negligence permitted the garbage of liberal Modernism to be presented as a gourmet meal to the young and innocent novice priests who originally entered seminary because they were attracted to the priesthood by the example of exquisitely faithful Catholic parents or the saints, or the Pope's holiness and courage, or the example of one of the many holy priests, or by Jesus Himself. Then they were sent from the seminary to spread the heresies and other false teachings, some that even smack of New Age beliefs. The condition in the Church today is described as a disaster — a sickness, and its poisonous cause is Modernism. Its sponsors are Judases!

Fr. Paul A. Wickens, in his booklet entitled *Christ Denied*, gives a scathing attack against Modernism. Wickens states that during the sessions of Vatican Council II the Modernist rhetoric "came out of the mouths of the left-wing faction of Vatican II, the French bishops, the Belgians, the Germans, joining ranks with the Canadian bishops and some midwestern prelates in America." Father Wickens states that the 32,000 priests who left the active priesthood were the products of the Modernist movement and "many of the bright American seminarians came back from their European indoctrination into Modernism and were placed into positions of great influence. Many became seminary professors, university officials, and indeed some became bishops."

Why is Modernism so attractive to so many bishops, priests, religious, and laity? Wickens says that in Modernism, the need for a prayer life is diminished. Much confusion reigns in the basic purpose of life, skepticism, uncertainty, and relativism of truth. You and God become one and your actions are God's actions. Therefore no need to examine your concience or go to Confession. It's not necessary to prepare for Holy Communion or be devoted to the saints. No meditation is necessary. The Modernists say that Vatican II eliminated all of these things. (*Christ Denied*, p. 29).

Wickens says on page 38 of his book that Modernism "sells well because it appeals to man's weaknesses, his sensuality, his pride, his sloth, while at the same time cloaking itself with the mantle of *new* spirituality."

Let's look at some other tenets of this condemned heresy called Modernism taken from Wickens book:

1) The Adam and Eve story is a myth.
2) We are not descended from Adam and Eve.
3) There is no such thing as Original Sin.
4) Modernists do not like laws that might limit their excesses and false teachings within the Church.

5) There is no Original sin so man is not a fallen race, therefore:
6) There is no hell and, therefore:
7) There is no Redeemer, therefore:
8) Jesus is not Divine (but we are because we are one with God).
9) Modernists are unhappy with regular or traditional prayer.
10) The Mass is not a sacrifice — only a meal and a memorial.
11) There is no true presence in the Eucharist.
12) Modernists do not like Confession but they like Communion.
13) Mass is not obligatory. There is no Primacy of Peter.
14) Christ was a teacher BUT NOT A SAVIOR.
15) They are not into apparitions or the supernatural!

Please bear with me for a few moments more on this limited but necessary commentary on Modernism, because what you are now going to read is the essence of why Modernism is so insidious, effective and rampant within the Church today among those you would never suspect and who are in the highest and most important positions ranging from pastor to bishop and among many, many nuns.

Again, the following is from Fr. Wickens book — *Christ Denied*, page 30. You will almost certainly be more attentive to the homilies and commentaries, writings and Church bulletins, guest speakers and visiting nuns, CCD lessons and Bible study classes, after you read these following words. Fr. Wickens says:

"This sort of heresy (Modernism) is very, very difficult to deal with. Pope Paul VI (during and after Vatican II) was hardpressed in combatting it, the bishops (loyal to Rome) were almost helpless in preventing its spread. Why? (and this is the clincher) Because when a Modernist talks about spirituality and the inner life he can, in effect, deny many doctrines without *appearing* to deny them. Thus, in condemning these modern movements, we appear to be condemning *sincere, well-meaning, Christ-oriented people*."

After reading that bombshell you can see why you and I must be alert as to what innovative things are going on in the Mass, in the words of the Consecration, in the liturgy in general, and what the children are hearing in their CCD classes. As an ex-school principal, I can tell you from personal experience, it is very difficult to control what goes on in that classroom when the door closes. I remember a phone call from a doctor who resented the fact that a 5th grade teacher told his daughter that she had her rights at home and didn't have to accept her parents' orders and rules. That teacher had just been placed on tenure by my predecessor, but you can imagine I watched her closely after that.

There was a teacher in Arizona a few years ago who was teaching CCD but she did not believe in the True Presence in the Eucharist. The system allowed the lady to fall "between the cracks" and she was teaching children of the parish. Who knows what she taught those children whom she was preparing for their First Holy Communion? So Vigilance! Ask questions! You are responsible for an adequate preparation of your children's souls and for the protection of your own. Don't assume everything is right and proper. If the priest is overly sensitive about your questions it might be because he himself is not sufficiently knowledgeable about the qualifications of his teaching staff. Although he is responsible under the Church, it's primarily the parents' responsibility to see that the true Faith and doctrine are being taught to their children. Ask and you shall receive. Inquire and you shall rest in conscience! Explain and the priest will repect you for your concern!

Words of Pope Paul VI (1977)

Words for you if you desire to be one of the faithful remnant.

"There is a great uneasiness, at this time, in the world and in the Church, and that which is in question, is the faith. It so happens now that I repeat to myself the obscure phrase of Jesus in the Gospel of St. Luke: 'When the Son of Man returns, will He still find faith on the earth?' It so happens that there are books coming out in which the faith is in retreat on some important points, that the episcopates are remaining silent and these books are not looked upon as strange. This, to me, is strange. I *sometimes read the Gospel passage of the end times and I attest that, at this time, some signs of this end-time are emerging.*

"Are we close to the end? This we will never know.

"We must always hold ourselves in readiness, but everything could last a very long time yet. What strikes me, when I think of the Catholic world, is that within Catholicism, there seems sometimes to predominate a non-Catholic way of thinking, and it can happen that this non-Catholic thought within Catholicism, w*ill tomorrow become the stronger.* But it will never represent the thought of the Church. It is necessary that *a small flock* subsist, no matter how small it might be." (Pope Paul VI)

So, dear reader, there is your challenge to be prepared for THE WARNING and its aftermath. There is your challenge to defend the Church and Jesus Christ Himself, against the horrors of the heresy of Modernism.

The Final Warning

CHAPTER FIVE
Jesus Speaks to Fr. Albert Drexel
Professor, Scientist, Mystic and Priest

This book contains only a fraction of the thousands of messages allegedly received by modern-day prophets. Most of these messages and warnings apply to the lay people of the world. The Mother of God, however has had some strong admonitions for priests as spoken to Father Gobbi since 1973. Another priest, Fr. Albert Drexel of Austria, began to receive messages from Jesus during the night of the First Friday of November, 1922 and they continued on every First Friday until a few days before his death in 1977. All of these messages concerned the Church and the consequences of those priests who have fallen into the heresy of Modernism and who still function as priests within the Church, intent on changing the traditional beliefs and doctrines to match their heretical notions of bringing the Church "up to date" in the modern world.

Fr. Drexel held three doctorates in philology and ethnology, was a victim-soul, and taught as a professor at the Vatican University for Missions. He had had a private audience with Pope Pius XI and served the Vatican in his field of expertise. Jesus spoke to him every First Friday night after which Fr. Drexel spent the entire night in prayer until seven in the morning when he resumed his official duties. He wrote a number of books, at least one of which was at the direction of Jesus Himself.

Fr. Drexel, himself a victim-soul and priest, writes in the strongest words of Jesus' concern for priests who are disloyal to the Magisterial teaching of the Church. The laity must always be on guard against erroneous teaching and practices in the Faith which could and do lead the innocent away from the One, True and Apostolic Church. You will appreciate more than ever those good, and holy priests, who, though fewer in number every year, still serve Jesus Christ as loyal sons, followers and teachers, when you experience and recognize those priests who have lost their Catholic Faith, and living the heresy of Modernism, continue to do harm internally within Mother Church.

It is with this intent — to alert you to the seriousness of conditions within the Church — that the following messages are presented. Remember as you read these words, they are, according to Father Drexel, the very words of Jesus Himself during our own times of the years 1970 to 1977. You will see the great love He has for His loyal and holy priests. You will see His hurt, anguish, disappointment and anger towards those consecrated sons who betray Him at His altar and in His plan of salvation.

Jesus accuses not only priests but even certain bishops who have deserted the Bark of Peter and through their casual leadership and loss of the true Faith are leading others to perdition. Since 1970 the Church has moved ever closer to the brink of schism. Our Lady of All Nations echoes the words of Jesus in Her messages recently approved by the Bishop of Haarlem, Holland. (See Chapter Eight for Mary's words).

The following messages are taken from the book *Faith is Greater Than Obedience*, published on March 2nd, 1976 by the Franciscan Minim Sisters of Mexico and translated from the German.

Fr. Drexel was in the process of writing a book highly critical of Modernism when Jesus spoke to him early in the morning of August 7, 1970. Jesus said:

"The makers of mischievousness in the Church started with My priests who are blessed servants and shepherds of My Church and because of the denial of Heaven and the supernatural which are the miracle of grace, they deify nature; therefore it is My special will that the writing you have done concerning the greatest heresy (Modernism) of the present time and also its originator, must appear in print and spread all over.

"The demolition of My one and true Church has not come to an end yet and will continue. The danger and destruction will increase until the day on which My visible Vicar in Rome shall speak the word of decision. Until that day the poison of corruption and unhindered confusion will do its destruction. Therefore, all of you continue to pray with great trust in the interceding power of My virginal Mother Mary, because by the grace of the Holy Trinity She was made conqueror of Satan and his demonic hordes, and OF HIS HUMAN SERVANTS AND HELPERS. [Emphasis by this author]

"So many of the faithful turned away from this wonderful Mother Mary under the influence of unfortunate priests who became disloyal servants of God; this will be not only their ruin, but also the ruin of the virtues of humility, purity and reverence in their lives. These poor, deceived and betrayed creatures abandon and forget the HEAVENLY FATHER, openly and in their hearts, and through whom I have taught the world and men to pray."

Words of the Savior in the Early Morning of Oct. 5, 1973:

"Pray especially to My Virgin Mother Mary. To My great joy I see that many people have taken up saying the Rosary. A great power dwells in this prayer. But others, on the other hand, among them priests, have set aside the Rosary, and have become tepid and cold interiorly. The result is desertion, the spirit of the world, turning away from the cross, wicked pride, and the sacrileges against the mystery and miracle of My Eucharistic Presence.

"For all honor given to Mary, Virgin and Mother, leads to Me, Her Son, and all graces flow from Me through the Heart and hands of My Mother to men. Therefore, She is called the Mediatrix, although it is I, Who have become the divine and only Mediator before the Eternal Father, through the bloody sacrifice of Golgotha.

"But is it not a terrible falsification, when more and more priests talk about a meal, but not of a sacrifice? Because without the mystical sacrifice of the altar, there would be no holy meal. Whoever acts and does not connect the sacrifice of the altar with My sacrifice of Golgotha, and priests who no longer believe in the miracle of consecration of bread and wine, make themselves GUILTY OF SIN, LIKE MY UNFORTUNATE APOSTLE JUDAS. They lie to themselves and become deceivers of the souls of the faithful people."

Words of the Savior in the morning of Dec. 7, 1973:

"Many bishops indulge heretical teachers, and they do not realize the duty of their ministry, and are realizing too late and are frightened, that they have betrayed the faith and the faithful people, in not protecting them from the wolves. However, they will not be able to overthrow My one and true Church because this Church shall rise again over moldy books of unbelief and immorality, and above the graves of heretical teachers. The prayer of the faithful shall triumph over the talks and gatherings of those who are cold in faith."

Words of the Savior in the morning of Feb. 1, 1974:

"Now My arch-enemy, Satan, with the help of consecrated priests and with theologians filled with pride, has plunged My Church into the most grave crisis of history, and many good and faithful sons and daughters of the Church hope and wish for interference from God and His omnipotence to silence the interior and exterior enemies of the Church... My ways are not your ways. The punishment for the enemies of God and for the destroyers and betrayers of My Church is enormous, and more terrible than any terrestrial catastrophe! Those who have been called to be My followers in the grace of consecration, and who have betrayed Me to the world, like Judas, shall go into the deepest hell, because terrible is the justice of God."

Words of the Savior in the morning of Mar. 1, 1974:

"A most difficult time for My one and true Church is near, because My sons called in My Church — the consecrated ones — have burdened themselves with three enormous and severe sins: the denial of My Divinity; the denial of My Resurrection; the denial of My presence in the mystery of the Host and the chalice by those who receive My Precious Blood. A threefold woe to these sins of unbelief, and a threefold curse upon those who make themselves guilty of even one of these!"

Words of the Savior in the morning of May 3, 1974:

"I tell you: there shall arise priests, who are now trained in hidden silence for the future and at the moment — and very soon — with apostolic spirit, following the footsteps of the saints, the discipline I desire and the unity of My Catholic Church, defending with holy reverence the mystery and miracle of the Holy Eucharist.

"Thus far rage the destroyers and their work of apostasy, but the ones who do it or let it happen, shall be judged. The judgement will be more severe for those who are My consecrated ones and who are called to guard the faith, but have not realized their ministry out of weakness.

"Because the apostate teachers, boasting of pride with their human knowledge, setting it in opposition to the Holy Ghost, forget that faith is a gift of grace, which is given to man through prayer and in an interior disposition turned truly to God. HOWEVER, this disposition begins with humility, gives witness through reverence, and flows into holy love."

Words of the Savior in the morning of Feb. 7, 1975:

"In addition to the desertion of God's commandments comes the desertion of the discipline of God. The guardian of this discipline is My visible successor in Rome. But there are priests who repudiate and oppose the office of the successor of Peter. In that way they are destroying My one and true Church from within, and this is the reason why the confusion could become so great. And at the same time these prophets of desertion are fighting against the Mother of the Church."

Words of the Savior in the morning of April 4, 1975:

"Only good priests can save the people in faith and keep them going in the spirit of prayer. My Heart and My love are longing for such priests. They should have: a strong and total faith; the spirit of prayer, and the desire of My Presence in the holy sacrifice; purity of heart and the overcoming of sensual inclinations against temptations. Only such priests are able to follow Me, the Lord and Master, in total surrender. Therefore, prayer for good priests is the great request of My Heart and the task of the believing people."

Words of the Savior in the morning of Dec. 5, 1975:

"The number of good priests is less, and the time is nearing in which many of the faithful people will be orphaned in their soul. Their home will become the dwelling place of the Church, wherein they, alone and together, will pray, and sing the praise of God. Spiritually, in love and with longing, they will foster the memory of the Blessed Sacrament and will receive Communion in a spiritual way... All those who will suffer under the trial in the coming difficult time, should inscribe in their heart the following three facts; First: holy and strong faith will give them interior peace and stability. This faith is a virtue and a grace which man can only preserve by prayer.

"Second: from faith, hope follows for an afterlife of eternity and the eternal happiness of contemplating God. For the true Christian the possession of this hope becomes a source of joy, which surpasses all worldly, earthly joys.

"Third: at My departure from this earth, before I entered into the glory of the Father, I spoke about love: he that keepeth My commandments, he it is that loveth Me. These commandments are commandments of the Triune God. Whoever meets Me in humility, reverence and sincerity in his daily life, loves Me, and if it would be only a quiet thought and in the ardent desire of the Blessed Sacrament, the miraculous bread of life. Out of love for Me, love for your neighbor will receive roots and nourishment.

"Once more I say: faith, hope, charity, those three! Attend school in the school of My most holy Mother; She is the teacher, intercessor, and mediatrix of grace!"

This chapter has consisted of the words of the Savior to Fr. Drexler. They fall into the category of *"tough love"* as used by today's psychologists and counselors when a loving but firm demand is made of their clients to change their lives before disaster strikes!

May God grant us the light to see those changes needed in all of us.

The Final Warning

CHAPTER SIX
Conchita

Conchita (Maria Concepion Cabrera de Armida of Mexico) was a mystic with her principal message on the Cross, the Church and the Trinity. Fr. M.M. Philipon, O.P., author of *Conchita* says she rivals St. Catherine of Siena and St. Teresa of Avila in the profoundness of her writings. She was a fiancee, mother and grandmother and died canonically as a religious without being deprived of her family status. She founded numerous religious organizations and died in 1937. The diocesan phase of the cause for her beatification has been completed.

Dec. 29, 1927:

Jesus to Conchita:

"As I have told you, there will come even worse times for My Church and she needs holy priests and ministers who will make her triumph over enemies, with the Gospel of peace, of forgiveness and charity; with My teaching of love which will overcome the world. But *I have need of an army of holy priests* transformed into Myself who exhale virtues and attract souls with the good aroma of Jesus Christ. I have need of other Christs on earth, forming one sole Christ in My Church through *unity of objectives, intentions and ideals, forming one only Mystical Body with Me, one only will with the will of My Father, one only Soul with the Holy Spirit, one unity with the Trinity, out of duty, out of justice, out of love.*"

Dec. 31, 1927:

"The transformation of the priest in Me which takes place in the Mass, *he must continue in his ordinary life, in order that this life be interior, spiritual and divine... Yet how many are the priests who do not think about this, who do not seek it, who make no effort to acquire it! They take on the incomparable dignity of the priesthood as if it were just an ordinary secular profession. Such is not the sublime and holy purpose of the priesthood which consists in perfect transformation into Me through love and through virtues.*"

Jan. 1, 1928:

"What is wanting in many of My priests is the spirit of mortification, love of the Cross, knowledge of its riches found in suffering. *Many preach the Cross but do not practice it.* They advise abnegation and self-renunciation but do not even dream of practicing those virtues so necessary for priests, for sacrifice is one of the culminating points and is the base for transformation into Me Who was a Victim from the very moment of My Incarnation onto My death.

"Thus then, a priest who wants to assimilate himself to Me, as is his obligation, must love sacrifice, must aspire to voluntary immolation, by devoting himself constantly on behalf of souls. Priest means one who offers himself and offers, who immolates himself and immolates. Priests must love the Cross and be in love with Me crucified. I am their model."

Mar. 28, 1928:

"Tell the Pope that it is My Will that in the whole Christian world, the Holy Spirit be implored to bring peace and His reign into hearts. Only this Holy Spirit will be able to renew the face of the earth. He will bring light, unity, and charity into hearts... *The world is foundering because it rejects the Holy Spirit and all the evils which afflict it have therein their origin...* May the whole world have recourse to this Holy

Spirit since the day of His reign has arrived. *This last stage of the world belongs very specially to Him that He be honored and exalted."*

Note: We see again that *priests are the key to the success of the plan of Jesus and Mary for the world.* Our obligation is clear — to pray for priests and bishops and for an abundance of priestly vocations and to heed the above words of Jesus in describing what He expects of His priests. As lay people, we also have the same obligation to love the Cross and immolate ourselves in love of God and neighbor.

The Final Warning

CHAPTER SEVEN
Christina Gallagher,
Fr. Gobbi, John Leary

THE WARNING

The Blessed Virgin Mary to Christina Gallagher of Ireland. She is
a victim soul and has founded a House of Prayer. Her spiritual
director is Fr. Gerard McGinnity, a theologian who believes strongly
that Christina's messages are from Heaven. He said, "The messages Christina Gallagher has received are *of the utmost seriousness, and should be looked upon in the light of similar messages
being given today by Our Lady in so many places, on every conti-
nent. As Christina points out, however, God will never force us, but
He is waiting for our response, while we still have time.*"

March 30, 1988:

"Tell all of My children of Ireland that they must pray, fast
and do penance, if there is to be peace. This can only be if
they respond to My call... My Son's hand is about to come
over the earth in justice." The following again shows our responsibility to help save souls.

THE WARNING

"There will come a sign, which everyone in the world, in an
interior way, will experience — and *it is not very far away.*
Everyone will experience an inner awareness and they *will
know* that this is from God, and they will see themselves as

---

they really are in the sight of God. *It is up to each one of us to help as many people as we can by our prayers, so that when this supernatural sign comes, they will change, and will be able to respond to that sign and be saved for God.*

"We must think not only of praying for our own souls and for our relatives and friends, *we must pray and make reparation for everyone, because that is what is expected of all believers, as God's children and members of Christ's Mystical Body. When we respond to God's grace, we can help others who cannot help themselves at that time, to be saved.*"

Note: From Christina's book *Please Come Back To Me and My Son:* "The chastisement has to come, to cleanse not only the world, but the Church, because the darkness is even in the Church." Mrs. Gallagher feels that time is short, believing *that everything she has been shown or told about, will be accomplished before the year 2000 is reached.*"

Jan. 30, 1991:

From Jesus: "My little one... tell all humanity to prepare themselves: the time has come for the cleansing of all humanity. A great darkness will come through the Son of God and man... My hand will come over the world more swiftly than the wind. Be not afraid... always unite yourself with Me, your Lord and Redeemer. I am your shield... Yes, you are nothing, but the work you permit Me to do through you is beyond your comprhending... the battle between light and darkness is great... I thirst for souls who will abandon themselves to Me... the Demons rage upon the earth... they are loosed from their pit. Tell all humanity of the Seven Seals of God... Seek only the Kingdom of God..."

Note: For those with a great interest and belief that we are in the End Times you need to acquire a copy of Fr. Gobbi's book *To The Priests-Our Lady's Beloved Sons.* This, in the opinion of many learned members of The Marian Movement of Priests, is one of the best guides available to lead us into the refuge of the Immaculate Heart of Mary and the Sacred Heart of Jesus.

Fr. Gobbi's book reveals the messages of Our Lady on topics such as the mark of The Beast, the significance of the numbers 666 as they relate to Satan, the coming time of the one world government during which period we will be asked to identify ourselves with the mark of the beast in order to purchase things, obtain a job, etc.

Our Lady states that *only the powerful force of prayer and reparative penance will be able to save the world* from what the justice of God has prepared for us. In his book, Mary confirms on Oct. 2, 1993, the warnings of a great fire from heaven described in her apparition at Akita, Japan. In Her messages of Dec. 31, 1992 Our Lady explains in detail that we *are in the End of Times,* Paragraph 485, page 801 of the 16th edition. . In this book Mary confirms the words of Christina Gallagher concerning **The Warning** cited above — when we will be enlightened by the Holy Spirit and see our souls as God sees us. She says we are a thousand times worse than the world was at the time of the great flood.

In Fr. Gobbi's book Mary again tells of the pastors who are in fear of exposing themselves to criticisms, and *who remain silent, no longer defending the flock which Christ has entrusted to them.* (par. 390, page 617, 16th edition) Mary asks that we live the Communion of Saints as we offer prayers for the poor souls in Purgatory who help us with their prayers and sufferings to survive the period of the Great Tribulation.

Fr. Gobbi's book can be obtained by writing to Rev. Albert G. Roux, P. O. Box 8, St. Francis, Maine 04774-0008. Include a small donation for your first book. Give your name and parish and ask to be listed as a member of the Marian Movement of Priests. There are no dues or other requirements except to try to attend a periodic cenacle of prayer in your area or to start a cenacle of two or more persons in your home. You will receive future editions of the book automatically. The book is also available in Spanish.

John Leary

Our final reference to recent heavenly messages is about those of John Leary, a chemist who works for the Kodak Company of

Rochester, New York. His spiritual director, Fr. Leo Klem, C.S.B. speaks highly of John as a person to whom God is speaking. John's messages are truly extraordinary in that they contain explicit details of the horrible circumstances under which we will be living, especially in the United States — circumstances that we will be facing "soon" according to Mr. Leary who has published eight volumes of his messages from Jesus and Mary. His books are titled *Prepare For The Great Tribulation and The Era of Peace.* (Available from Queenship Publishing.)

Notice that Mr. Leary speaks of an era of peace, as does every visionary or locutionist whose messages are cited above. Mary's Heart will triumph, She says, by the Golden Jubilee Year of 2000, at which time we will live in a period of peace for a time. The Holy Father has said we are heading for a wonderful time of peace in God and we should be preparing during these years of 1997 though 1999 with special study and prayer for the coming of that time of peace. But first, the modern prophets say we are to pass through the tribulation and chastisement — a period of purification for the terrible transgressions of mankind, including the Church, before we enter into that time of peace.

June 12, 1996:

God the Father speaks: "My good people, as you saw Me come before My prophet Elijah, so I go before My prophets of your day to give witness of My power in them. No prophet claims any power of their own, but it is by My working in them that you will recognize these signs of My Presence.

"My children, listen to My words in Scripture for your lesson in how to live life. I have given you My commandments through Moses, to order your life before Me and your neighbor. See, even now I am listening for your response to My Word, by how you act in life. Give Me praise and glory each day, so you can witness your love for Me and your thanks for all I have given you.

"Listen to My Son, Jesus, Who has gone before you to give you an example of how to live. I have sent My Son as an offering for your sins and a Savior to bring you to Me. Pray and I will bring you My grace to lead a faithful life to My commands."

Jesus speaks: "My people, you see things up close in your own small portion of the world. I wish that you would think more of the big picture of how your life fits in with all of those around you. As you think more beyond yourself, you can understand what is more important in your world and more important to Me. I ask you *to help your neighbor more without being asked, and to do these things for Me, not just for your own selfish interests.*

"My people, your justice system becomes more corrupt as it loses more respect for life. Your abortion laws are an example of your corrupt justice. As you hold any life vulnerable to be disposed of, you are putting everyone's life on the line. Even now, men are striving to end people's lives who feel they wish someone to help them in state-assisted suicide. Soon, people will decide further who who will live and who will die. Once you start this cycle, no one is sacred. Fight now against these laws or you will all be consumed by them.

"I have told you I will prepare a place for you after death, **but I will prepare a place, also, here on earth after My purification. After the conquest of Satan, you will see Me renew the earth.** For those who are faithful, I will bring you to a world of peace and love with no fighting, no drugs, no pollution, and no death. Everything will be in harmony with My Will. Even the animals will not attack each other, since food will not be necessary for survival.

"My people, many will see hardships through the chastisements of your weather. They will be brought to their knees as their way of living will be threatened. Some have *still not realized that their sins are calling for this reparation.* Come to Me in prayer, My children, for prayer is an easier answer to your society's problems. Do something now to ward off My wrath or these happenings will increase in severity."

June 15, 1996:

Jesus speaks: "My people, the day of reckoning for the earth is at hand. Soon My angels will make their presence known, as you will be visited with My many plagues as in the Exodus. **You will see locusts, grasshoppers, and other pestilences ravage your crops. Diseases of all various kinds will follow, both for plants and animals. With these plagues, will come a great famine over the land.** Your faith will protect you. All of these chastisements will be sent to purify the earth of man's worship of alien gods. All of your possessions will be gradually stripped from you, so you are fully dependent on Me instead of yourselves. As man consents My power is greater than his own he will come on his knees to acknowledge God. Keep faith in Me and you will find My Heaven on earth."

CHAPTER EIGHT

Messages and Warnings: Our Lady of All Nations, Our Lady of the Light, Fr. Gobbi, Jacinta

This chapter offers some of the messages from apparitions or locutions which are related in some way to THE WARNING — that experience wherein all people will see the true condition of their souls as enlightened by the Holy Spirit. This astounding, and perhaps frightening experience, has been predicted at Akita, Garabandal, in Ireland, and the U. S.

Each of these messages will be identified by location, date, and name of the visionary or locutionist and whether the alleged supernatural event has been approved for belief by the faithful or if it is still under investigation by the Church. The investigation is almost always left to the local Ordinary (Bishop). If any such occurrence teaches against Catholic faith and morals the substance of the messages are condemned by the Church and Catholics are forbidden to physically visit the site. None of these messages which follow have been condemned.

Please keep in mind that Canon Law of the Church permits the acceptance and propagation of alleged supernatural messages as long as they have not been condemned, and books such as the one you are reading no longer require official approval through the Imprimatur so long as nothing therein teaches against faith and morals.

The long delays in official Church approval resulted in serious problems for the world. The apparitions at Fatima, Portugal were finally approved after fourteen years of study by the Church. As a consequence, few cooperated with Mary's requests for prayer and penance, and — as she predicted would happen if sufficient people did not comply — atheistic communism and World War II struck as forms of chastisement. She had stated that WW I was a chastisement for mankind's sins and a worse punishment would be forthcoming if the world did not return to God and the living of the Ten Commandments and return to prayer and penance. Look at the condition of the state of morality today; crime, abortion, murder, wars, sins against purity, and white collar crime, and we can see the degradation of the world in quantum leaps since WW II. *Little Jacinta*, as she was lying in the hospital shortly before she died stated clearly and with anguish that Mary told her of the great need for our doing penance: "Our Lady said that there are many wars and disputes in the world; but wars are only the punishment for the sins of the world. The Blessed Virgin can no longer hold back the arm of Her Son over the world. *There must be amendment. If men repented of their sins, Our Lord would forgive them, but if they do not change their life, THE CHASTISEMENT WILL COME."*

Our Lady of All Nations — May 31, 1965 to Ida Peerdeman in Amsterdam. Approved by Bishop Hendrik Bomers of Haarlem, Holland:

> "Go to the Pope and tell him in the name of the Lady of All Nations this is the last warning before the end of the Council (Vatican Council II). The Church of Rome is in danger of a schism. Warn your priests. Let them put a stop to those false theories about the Eucharist, sacraments, doctrine, priesthood, marriage, and family-planning. They are being led astray by the spirit of untruth — Satan — and confused by the idea of modernism. Divine teaching and laws are valid for all time and newly applicable to every period... the Church of Rome must remain the Church of Rome."

May 31, 1956:

> "Tell the sacristan to the Holy Father that he should indicate to him that *celibacy still is the great strength of the Church..."*

May 31, 1957:

"Go to the Holy Father and tell him that I have said: the time has now arrived for the Dogma to be proclaimed. (Mary is co-redemptrix, advocate and mediatrix) I shall come back privately at the time chosen by the Lord to assist the Church and the priests. Say that *celibacy is endangered from within, but the Holy Father must always uphold it notwithstanding all opposition."*

Feb. 14, 1950:

"There is a strong tendency in the world towards what is good and this is just why the other spirit is at work. That spirit is busy influencing and corrupting the world. Mankind is not bad in itself, but weak. Do you see that crucifix? To this man-kind will have to be brought back. I ask them urgently, in this modern world with its technology, *not to forget that simple cross!"*

Our Lady of the Light, **Oct. 26, 1992 in Cold Spring, Kentucky.**

The visionary desires to remain anonymous but is under the spiritual direction of Fr. R. Leroy Smith, pastor of St. Joseph Church in Cold Spring, Ky. His spiritual life went through vast changes after a visit to Medjugorje in Oct. 1988. Mary is said to be directing personal messages to him and allegedly selected him for her plans in Cold Spring.

Our Lady has told the visionary in Cold Spring that the chastisements she speaks of will be revealed to some as such, but that others will not recognize them as chastisements. She also revealed that each one, in his own heart, will know they are being chastised for the Holy Spirit shall reveal it to them. About the WARNING Our Lady said, "Soon a time will come when each one shall undergo a personal and individual view into their own soul, and they will see their weakness and their falsehoods. *Every soul shall undergo this with no exceptions. Then, they will have a choice!"*

Note: The Blessed Mother always insists on an increase in prayer to bring about our conversion, a change in our direction back to God. In the following words She offers some very specific guidance to help us make these changes in our spiritual and everyday lives.

Oct. 26, 1992:

"My child, I pointed out to you that in Fatima during the early part of this century, I also came as Our Lady of Light and the reference to the *New Era* had already begun even then. *All of My appearances, then and since then, are connected together, for I am the same Lady, and my messages are the same. As at Fatima, so it is now. You are thinking in man's time, not God's. Be patient, for all shall unfold on schedule, but in God's time.* Know that all of my appearances in every part of the earth are part of a plan for the salvation of mankind. It is, therefore, requested that all should be recorded and retained. Yes, these will be the additional scriptures. Both private and public appearances are necessary to draw my children back to God, so both are important and should be recorded. In the discernment of these appearances, you shall know the truth by the *forthcoming fruits of each event. The truth shall be revealed in the bearing of the fruit.*

"It is the time of fulfillment of many Scriptures as well as the unfoldment of my messages to My children on earth through the Fatima Messages. I urge all of you to continue to pray the Rosary and to urge all of your brothers and sisters to do so also. In this way I can continue to intervene and forestall, if not eliminate the catastrophic events to befall earth as a chastisement for their errors."

Feb. 9, 1992:

"It is not the Father's plan or desire to do this, but mankind has brought these events upon himself by his pride and greed... I have given you the means and shown you the way but you do not budge. I plead with you... *for the TIME GROWS SHORT.*

"You must rid yourselves of falsehoods and live a life that is united to God... Give yourself fully to Him; your possessions, all of your desires, and relinquish your will to do His Holy Will... Open yourself to God's unconditional love.

"Above all I desire that you love one another...

"I desire that you quit judging your brothers and sisters...

"I desire that you quit looking with contempt on those less fortunate than you.

"I desire that you quit raising youselves above others, for in the family of God... there are none better and none less.

"I also desire that you quit holding grudges against each other...

"Remember, dear children, you cannot come to the Father if you harbor these impurities in your spirit. You must have a pure heart so that you present no falsehood. You must learn to pray with all your heart and all your might. *For a prayer from a pure heart is stronger than any force you know on earth...* My children, if you do not speak to the Father now, how will He know you when you come into the spiritual world before Him? ... There is nothing you have done or will do that has not been forgiven you through the death of My Son, Jesus, on the Cross... Pray, fast, convert, and reconcile with one another. I urge you to consecrate yourselves to My Immaculate Heart and to the Sacred Heart of My Son.

"Do not waste your time for time is running out... Start today to love one another. When asked by others what they can do, tell them to live My messages and be examples to others of how to live a holy life..."

Fr. Stefano Gobbi

The Blessed Mother to Fr. Stefano Gobbi in Malvern, Pennsylvania on Nov. 15, 1990. He has received locutions from Mary since 1973. His book contaning the messages from Our Lady has been granted the Imprimatur of the Church. His book *To The Priests - Our Lady's Beloved Sons* is written for the members of the Marian Movement of Priests; those priests, religious, and laity who are loyal to Mary, the Holy Father in Rome, and the Magisterial teaching of the Church.

The Blessed Virgin to Fr. Gobbi:

"Abortions — these killings of innocent children that cry out for vengeance before the Face of God — have spread and are performed in every part of your homeland (USA). The moment of Divine Justice and of Great Mercy has now arrived. *You will know the hour of weakness and of poverty, the hour of suffering and defeat; the purifying hour of the Great Chastisement.*"

CHAPTER NINE
La Salette, Fatima, Sr. Faustina, Garabandal, Akita, Medjugorje and Betania

La Salette, France — 1846 (Approved by the Church)

The Blessed Virgin appeared to two children to give these warnings:

"If my people do not submit themselves (their will to God) I will be forced to let go of the hand of my Son."

"God will strike in an unprecedented way. Woe to the inhabitants of the earth! God will exhaust His wrath upon them and no one will be able to escape so many afflictions together. Everywhere there will be extraordinary wonders as true Faith has faded and false light brightens the people."

"The Vicar of my Son will suffer a great deal, because for a while the Church will yield to a large persecution, a time of darkness and the Church will witness a frightful crisis..."

"A forerunner of the Antchrist, with his troops gathered from several nations, will fight against the true Christ, the only Savior of the world. He will shed much blood and will want to annihilate the worship of God, to make himself looked upon as a god."

"The earth will be struck by calamities of all kinds in addition to plagues and famines which will be widespread. There will be a series of wars until the last war, which will be fought by the Ten Kings of the Antichrist (Rev. 17:12), all of whom will have one and the same plan and will be the only rulers of the world. Before this comes to pass, there will be a false peace in the world. People will think of nothing but amusement. The wicked will give themselves over to all kinds of sin. But the children of the Holy Church, the children of my Faith, my true followers, will grow in their love for God and in all the virtues precious to me..."

"The seasons will be altered, the earth will produce nothing but bad fruit, the stars will lose their regular motion, the moon will reflect a reddish glow. Water and fire will give the earth's globe convulsions and terrible earthquakes which will swallow up mountains and cities...

"Rome, the city, will lose the Faith and become the seat of the Antichrist." (Rev. 17)

"The demons of the air together with the Antichrist will perform great wonders on earth and in the atmosphere (Rev. 13:13), and men will become more and more perverted. The Church will be in eclipse, the world will be in dismay... *Fire will fall and consume three cities. All the universe will be struck with terror and many will let themselves be led astray because they have not worshipped the true Christ who lives among them.* It is time; the sun is darkening; only Faith will survive."

Fatima, Portugal — 1917 (Approved by the Church)

The Blessed Mother appeared to three young children and gave these warnings after asking them if they were willing to offer themselves to God and bear all their sufferings as an act of reparation for the sins by which He is offended, although at the same time, the grace of God would be their comfort.

After showing the children a vision of hell and the suffering of the souls there, Mary said:

"You have seen where the souls of poor sinners go. To save them, God wishes to establish in the world devotion to my Immaculate Heart. If what I say to you is done, many souls will be saved and there will be peace... If my requests are heeded, Russia will be converted and there will be peace; *if not she will spread her errors* [of atheistic communism] *throughout the world causing wars and persecutions of the Church. The good will be martyred, the Holy Father will have much to suffer, and various nations will be annihilated."*

Blessed Sister Faustina (Beatified by the Church) 1931-1938

To this holy nun, Jesus taught the truth of His boundless Mercy for every person and shared with her the Chaplet of Mercy in preparation for the "end times" and its tribulations and persecutions of members of the Church. In order to make His forgiving and merciful love universally known, Our Lord called for a Feast of Divine Mercy to be celebrated in the whole Church. He said to Sister Faustina:

"I desire that the Feast of Mercy be a refuge and shelter for all souls and especially for poor sinners. On that day the very depths of My tender Mercy are open. I pour out a whole ocean of graces upon those souls who approach the Fount of My Mercy. The soul that will go to Confession and receive Holy Communion shall obtain complete forgiveness of sins and punishment. Let no soul fear to draw near to Me and though its sins be as scarlet, My Mercy is so great that no mind, be it of man or angel, will be able to fathom it throughout eternity..."

So, in spite of severe warnings of a possible chastisement, God offers His forgiveness to those in need of His Mercy, and He offers it so generously!

Garabandal, Spain – 1961-1965 (Under study by the Church)

The Blessed Virgin Mary and St. Michael the Archangel appeared to four young girls in the isolated mountain village of

Garabandal. The messages given to the children are much the same as Fatima and La Salette. The Blessed Mother told the girls:

> "We must make many sacrifices, perform much penance, and visit the Blessed Sacrament frequently, but first we must lead good lives. If we do not, a chastisement will befall us. The cup is already filling up and if we do not change, a very great punishment will come upon us."

On December 8, 1964, the Blessed Mother told one of the children that St. Michael would appear and he would give another message on June 18, 1965. St. Michael spoke in the name of the Blessed Virgin Mary saying on June 18th:

> "As my message of October 18, 1961 has not been complied with and has not been made known to the world, I am advising you that this is the last one. Before, the cup was filling up. Now it is spilling over. *Many clergy are on the road to perdition and are taking many souls with them. Less and less importance is given to the Eucharist.* You should turn the wrath of God away from yourselves by your efforts. If you ask His forgiveness with sincere hearts, He will pardon you. I, your Mother, through the intercession of St. Michael, the Archangel, ask you to amend your lives. You are now receiving the last warnings. I love you very much, and I do not want your condemnation. Pray to us with sincerity and we will grant your requests. You should make more sacrifices. Think about the Passion of Jesus."

The WARNING!

The Blessed Mother promised three separate acts from God: a WARNING, a great MIRACLE, and a CHASTISEMENT. *The warning will allow every soul on earth to see their soul the way God sees them no matter what a person's religion is.* Every person alive will see the results of their sins and how those sins affected God and neighbor. The warning is for our own good to draw us to Jesus and the Father. It is a great sign of God's mercy in that nonbelievers will see there is a God when they experience the warning, and will be given a chance to change and return to God by living the Ten Commandments, as will the believers!

Akita, Japan — 1973-1981 (Approved by the Church)

These apparitions are among the most interesting because the local bishop, Bishop Ito, saw the supernatural phenomena which took place in the little convent of Akita, Japan. Sister Agnes Sasagawa was healed of her deafness, saw the signs of Angels before the Blessed Sacrament in the tabernacle of the altar, heard the Blessed Mother speak to her, received the wounds of Christ in her hands, and saw, with all the nuns, the statue of the Blessed Virgin Mary cry human tears 101 times. The Bishop himself saw the tears on four different occasions. The statue also shed tears of blood and blood seeped from a wound in the shape of a cross in the hand of the image which was carved from wood. Mary's warning in Akita is very ominous:

"Pray very much for the Pope, bishops, and priests... Many men in this world afflict the Lord. I desire souls to console Him to soften the anger of the Heavenly Father. I wish, with my Son, for souls who will offer their suffering and their poverty for the conversion of sinners and ingrates."

"In order that the world might know His anger, the Heavenly Father is preparing to inflict a great chastisement on all mankind. With my Son, I have prevented the coming of calamities by offering Him the sufferings of the Son on the Cross, His Precious Blood and beloved souls who console Him, forming a cohort of victim souls. Prayer, penance, and courageous sacrifices can soften the Father's anger..."

"As I told you, if men do not repent and better themselves, the Father will inflict a terrible punishment greater than the deluge... *Fire will fall from the sky and will wipe out a great part of humanity, the good as well as the bad, sparing neither priests nor the faithful. The survivors will find themselves so desolate that they will envy the dead! The only arms which will remain for you will be the Rosary and the Sign left by my Son. Each day recite the Rosary, pray for the Pope, the bishops, and the priests."*

Medjugorje, Yugoslavia — 1981-1997 (Under study by the Church):

The Blessed Mary Virgin began to speak to six young children, two boys and four girls. The messages have a great sense of urgency about them, emphasizing the need for the whole world to "come back to God" and "all who leave this place, when you return home, live your faith devoutly, whatever your faith."

Mary asks for 1) conversion to God, 2) daily prayer, 3) faith, 4) fasting and 5) peace and reconciliation. Mary said that if the world does not return to God, a great chastisement will befall us. Over 19 million people have visited the site at Medjugorje, including thousands of priests, and even some bishops. Many healings have taken place and thousands of conversions. Amazing phenomena have been seen, such as a spinning sun, a spinning and shining cross and some are reported to have been captured on film and on video. Our Blessed Mother said, "Pray and fast, and I will pray with you, and Jesus will grant your requests." Our requests, of course, should be for those spiritual things we need and a seeking for the Kingdom of God — and "all the rest will be given" to us.

Betania, Venezuela — 1976-1997 (Approved by the Church):

A Eucharistic Miracle took place in Betania during Mass. This has been approved by the Church as a supernatural event. Maria Esperanza, a visionary to whom Mary is alleged to appear says that Mary has shown herself to thousands of pilgrims at the apparition site. Mary appears under the title of Our Lady of Reconciliation. The messages here warn of a great chastisement if the people of the world do not return to living the commandments of God.

CHAPTER TEN
Prayers and Comments

Psalm 90

O Lord, You have been our refuge from one generation to the next.
Before the mountains were born on the earth or the world brought
forth, You are God, without beginning or end.

You turn men back into dust and say: "Go back, sons of men,"
To Your eyes a thousand years are like yesterday, come and gone,
No more than a watch in the night.

You sweep men away like a dream. like grass which springs up in
the morning. In the morning it springs up and flowers:
By evening it withers and fades.

So we are destroyed in Your anger, struck with terror in Your fury.
Our guilt lies open before You; our secrets in the light of Your face.

All our days pass away in Your anger. Our life is over like a sigh.
Our span is seventy years or eighty for those who are strong.

And most of these are emptiness and pain. They pass swiftly and
we are gone. Who understands the power of Your anger and fears
the strength of Your fury?

Make us know the shortness of our life that we may gain wisdom
of heart.
Lord, relent! Is Your anger forever? Show pity to Your servants.

In the morning, fill us with Your love; we shall exult and rejoice all our days. Give us joy to balance our affliction for the years when we knew misfortune.

Show forth Your work to Your servants; let Your glory shine on their children. Let the favor of the Lord be upon us: Give success to the work of our hands, give success to the work of our hands.

Prayer requested by Our Lady of All Nations in Holland:

"Lord Jesus Christ, Son of the Father, send now Your Spirit over the earth.
Let the Holy Spirit live in the hearts of all nations, that they may be preserved from degeneration, disaster, and war.
May the Lady of All Nations, who once was Mary, be our Advocate. Amen.

Message from Our Lady of Medjugorje on Jan. 25, 1997 :

"Dear Children! I invite you to reflect about your future. You are creating a new world without God, with only your strength and that is why you are unsatisfied and without joy in the heart. This time is My time and that is why, little children, I invite you again to pray. When you find unity with God, you will feel hunger for the word of God and your heart, little children, will overflow with joy. You will witness God's love wherever you are. I bless you and I repeat to you that I am with you to help you. Thank you for having responded to My call."

Prayer For Priests

Many of the messages cited in the previous chapters have spoken rather boldly, although with compassion, about those priests who are not living the Catholic Faith. We hope that those words are addressed to an absolute minimum of priests who need to hear the critical words of Jesus and Mary. Only the reader knows to what extent, through personal experience, the priests of their acquaintance have become the target for Our Lord's warnings. But we know that Jesus loves all of us, no matter what our track record reveals about us, and He wants every priest and layman to be saved. He makes it clear, however, that all of us have a tremendous responsibility to pray for others, but especially for priests who are the backbone of the Church. We should, in the crisis facing the Church — not only because of the shortage of priests, but also because of the number who are falling away from the true Catholic Faith — never fail to offer sincere prayers on behalf of all priests; for their conversion, protection from evil, and preservation of their vocation. For those who are loyal to the Holy Father, Mary, and the magisterial teaching of the Church we should go out of our way to show our appreciation and offer encouragement. It takes heroic courage to adhere to the traditional teachings of the Church in the face of the ridicule, scorn, and contempt they suffer from some of the laity and their own brothers in the priesthood. It is like a martyrdom of sorts for them if they never see the fruits of their loyalty and courage, or the approval of the faithful flock.

How many of us could live the lonely life of a priest under the conditions of today with criticism from every quarter, including their own brother-priests? Those priests who are teaching error, including heresy, especially need our prayers.

They also need to be informed if they are wrong, preferably from their superiors. Nowadays, some of the superiors are as much in error as the subordinate priests. They also should be made aware that they will not receive the financial support of the people so long as they are deviating from the one and true Catholic Faith in the teaching of the flock.

Every Catholic is obligated to speak out in correction of anyone teaching errors against the Faith, as pronounced by the Blessed Virgin Mary to Fr. Gobbi in Dallas, Texas on Dec. 3, 1986. The Blessed Mother said, "You must oppose anyone who teaches doctrines which are different and, above all, you must speak openly to all the faithful of the grave danger, which they are encountering today, of swerving from the true faith in Jesus and His Gospel!"

That message was given eleven years ago! Things have gone downhill considerably in the Church sine 1986. We are on the brink of schism in this country (according to a message to Fr. Gobbi from Our Lady).

Prayer, penance, fasting, confession, and the living of the Ten Commandments are the strongest weapons against the diabolic activities focused on the Church, and Our Lady says there isn't much time remaining to help Her turn conditions around. She promises that in the end, Her Immaculate Heart will triumph and we can believe that! Jesus said the Gates of Hell would not prevail against His Church and we can believe that with absolute confidence!

We must pray for the conversion of priests and we must pray for our own conversion. The weak faith and sins of the laity and clergy are the causes of the coming warning and chastisement. God have mercy on us all.

PART TWO

THE REMNANT
How To Preserve Your Catholic Faith

The Final Warning

INTRODUCTION

Part I, *The Final Warning-A Defense Against Modernism,* was written to hopefully assist the average layperson to recognize the great threat in the Church today. The heresy of Modernism, assisted by rationalism, is bringing the Church to the brink of schism and the loss of millions of souls who are ignorant of this threat.

This part is offered as an assist in practical actions available within the power and resources of any Catholic who desires to be a member of the REMNANT Christ spoke about — the remnant that will bravely live and fight to preserve the Faith founded by Jesus Christ and become one of Mary's cohorts in the Triumph of Her Immaculate Heart.

The faithful members of the hierarchy, along with the Holy Father recognize that the Church is in a downward spiral of disintegration and impotence caused by the inroads of Modernism and liberal Church leaders, including some cardinals and many bishops. The Pope has recognized that we are close to or in fact are in the time of the Great Apostasy, a turning away from God and His Kingdom. His Kingdom on earth has been for two thousand years, the Roman Catholic Church. But this Kingdom is barely a shadow of its former self before Vatican Council II. The primary cause of the Church's condition is the liberal movement which gained extraordinary power and momentum during the period of the Council and has gained strength daily.

The primary contributor to this situation is the deterioration of many of the Catholic seminaries that are controlled by the Modernists and liberals, producing too many confused and misdirected priests, who, for the most part, and with few exceptions, would never recognize the orthodox Faith as it was taught up until

Vatican II. Those of us who lived that ancient and magnificent Catholic doctrine are now the outsiders, the spiritual squares who are behind the times, the old-fashioned unsophisticated who believe in miracles and all aspects of the supernatural and who believe in the dogmas and doctrines taught and handed down through the centuries as part of the official doctrine and traditions of the Roman Catholic Church. The faithful remnant are now the "bad guys", and the deserters of the true Faith are now the "good guys." We need to become a Catholic Church once again!

Dr. Malachai has said that the situation in the Church is critical. Some of those "in charge" of the Church, holding resposible positions of leadership, are not only guilty of heresy, but of apostasy. They have lost the faith completely, and are in "the drivers seat." The faithfull remnant is up against Goliath, but as part of the Blessed Mother's cohort, will triumph with her Immaculate Heart — but only after a tremendous battle!

Feast of the Queenship of Mary
August 22, 1997

CHAPTER ONE
The Catholic Church is Under Siege

Our Catholic Faith is under the worst attack in its history because it has been under direct attack by Satan for the past 100 years. Pope Leo XIII said that God had permitted him to see in a vision that Satan was given the power and authority to persecute the Church in a special way for about one hundred years. We are coming to the end of this 100 year period as we approach the Golden Jubilee Year of 2000 at which time the Holy Father says we will embark upon a long period of peace and glory for the Church. Satan, realizing that his time is short, has entered into the Church in a real way.

Although special power was given to Satan to try to destroy Christ's Church, he would be totally impotent if he had no one to do his bidding. But he has — *and he has the very ones who vowed to serve Christ and His Church and who are deserting those vows, the Magisterium, and the Blessed Mother.* The prophet Jeremiah speaks — *"Woe to the shepherds who mislead and scatter the flock of my pasture says the Lord.* Therefore, thus says the Lord, the God of Israel, against the shepherds who shepherd My people: *You have scattered my sheep and have driven them away. You have not cared for them, but I will take care to punish your evil deeds.* **I myself will gather the remnant of My flock from all the lands** to which I have driven them and bring them back to My meadow; there they will increase and multiply, and I will appoint shepherds for them who will shepherd them so they will no longer fear and tremble; none shall be missing says the Lord." — Jer. 23:1-6

Jeremiah's words still speak with fire and threat to those liberals and Modernists who have decided they know better than the

Magisterium, better than the Holy Father who is Mary's hand-picked
pontiff, better than the saints of the Church who lived heroic lives
to teach and preach, and suffer and die to preserve this one, holy,
catholic and apostolic faith for this very generation which is, for
the most part, abandoning it. And they are abandoning it under the
misleading and erroneous leadership of the modern Judases who
are undermining this Church from within.

These are the Judases who are betraying their Master today by
teaching there is no True Presence in the Eucharist. Approximately
80% of so-called practicing Catholics seem to agree. This founda-
tional doctrine of the Eucharist is fast fading into oblivion among
those who still insist they are Roman Catholic. In matters of theology, it is not what the majority says that rules. Truth is truth and no
number of theologians or lay supporters can change the truth because they will to change the truth.

The aim and purpose of the false leaders and stupified followers is to water down the Catholic Faith until it will make no differ-
ence whether one is Protestant or Catholic. This Most Holy Gift to
the Catholic Church is now treated as if Jesus had never granted us
this gift of HIMSELF. To them it is only a symbol — again reflect-
ing our Protestant brothers' belief about the Eucharist. They ignore the Gospel and invent their own rationalization to explain away
the True Presence. But, in order to do that they must first abandon
the Gospel itself. Read here, dear friends, what the Savior Himself
taught His first priests — His apostles.

"I Myself am the Living Bread come down from heaven. If
anyone eats this Bread he shall live forever: **the Bread I will
give is My flesh, for the life of the world... Let Me sol-
emnly assure you, if you do not eat the flesh of the Son of
Man and drink His blood, you have no life in you. He
who feeds on My flesh and drinks My blood remains in
Me, and I in him.** Just as the Father Who has life sent Me
and I have life because of the Father, *so man who feeds on
Me will have life because of Me.* This is the Bread that came
down from heaven. Unlike your ancestors who ate and died
nonetheless, the man who feeds on this Bread shall live forever." — John 6:57

As Catholics we believe in and accept the Bible and we believe in the words of Jesus in that Bible. Are we now to understand that the Modernists and liberals are skipping through the Bible and rejecting that with which they disagree? Are we then also to believe that *they have no life in them* since they reject the belief in the TRUE PRESENCE? Of course, here we are speaking of supernatural life, the life of grace and the life of the soul. Are we to understand that *they no longer remain in Jesus and He in them?* If we accept Jesus' words literally then are we to believe that about 80% of Roman Catholics are depriving themselves of this supernatural life? It is difficult to think otherwise! But it is not difficult to see why so many problems (divorce, broken families, poor Church attendance and pathetically poor participation in the Sacrament of Reconciliation) are plaguing the Catholic laity and the clergy. The proliferation of Eucharistic Miracles in the Church today is a sign of the times and a gift from Jesus to draw all of us back to the miraculous sacrifice — the Holy Eucharist.

St. Peter Julian Eymard, founder of the Priests of the Blessed Sacrament says the following about the need for the Blessed Sacrament:

> "I am not afraid to say it: the cult of Solemn Exposition is the great need of our times: this public and solemn profession of faith in the divinity of Christ and in the reality of His Sacramental Presence is a necessity. It is the best refutation which can be leveled at the renegades, the apostates, the impious and the indifferent. It will crush them like a mountain of fire, but a fire of love and goodness.
>
> "This solemn cult of exposition is also necessary to arouse the slumbering faith of many good people who have forgotten Jesus Christ, because they have lost sight of the fact that He is their neighbor, their friend, and their God.
>
> "The great evil of the day lies in the fact that we don't go to Jesus as to a Savior and a God. We abandon the only basis, the only law, the only grace of salvation. The trouble about empty piety is that it fails to spring from Jesus Christ, or terminate in Him. People stop or loiter on the way. A divine love which does not derive its fervor, its center, in the Sacra-

ment of the Holy Eucharist, lacks the essential conditions of power. It will soon die out like the hearth without fuel. This love will soon become merely human.

"What then, must we do? Go back to the source of life which is Jesus. But we must cease viewing Jesus only in His earthly life or in the glory of Heaven: we must see Him especially in the Holy Eucharist. We must take Him from the back seat and place Him at the head of our Christian civilization, which He will guide and bring to safety. We must rebuild His palace, a royal throne, a court of devoted servants, a family of friends, a people of adorers.

"Behold the mission and the glory of our age: that will make it the greatest and holiest of centuries..."

The Pope Speaks On The Eucharist:

Quoting St. Peter Julian Eymard and the Holy Father is unlikely to convince any of those who do not believe in the supernatural. How could they believe in the Miracle of the Altar? These words are more for those who are going to be the Remnant — to support your faith and loyalty and to predict the glorious outcome awaiting those who remain loyal to Jesus, Mary, and the Holy Father, who, on June 1st, 1997 spoke at the Eucharistic Congress in Wroclaw, Poland:

"The Church lives by the Eucharist; she draws from it the spiritual energy to carry out her mission. It is the Eucharist that gives her the strength to grow and be united. **The Eucharist is the heart of the Church**... In the Upper Room Jesus effects the consecration. By virtue of His words, **the bread, while keeping the external appearance of bread, becomes His Body, and the wine becomes His Blood.** This is the great mystery of faith! . . We are sharers in the saving mystery of Christ and we await His coming in glory. Through the institution of the Eucharist, we have entered into the end times, the time of awaiting Christ's Second Coming, when the world will be judged and at the same time the work of redemption will be brought to completion. The Eucharist does not merely speak of all this. In the Eucharist all this is celebrated in it — all this is fulfilled. Truly the Eucharist is the great sacrament of the Church. The Church celebrates the Eucharist, and at the same time the **EUCHARIST MAKES THE CHURCH!**"

Those are the words of the Vicar of Christ on earth — he is "Peter." He is speaking for Christ on earth. But who is listening? Is it possible that Catholic clergy and laity can walk away from the belief in the True Presence and still claim to be Catholic? Is it possible that clergy and laity can scoff at the papal encyclicals and call themselves Catholic? In a homily in Tucson, Arizona, in 1996, the popular guest on Mother Angelica's T. V. program — Fr. Groeschel, said, "NO, ABSOLUTELY NOT. WE CANNOT CALL OURSELVES CATHOLIC if we do not adhere to and obey the encyclical teachings of the Holy Father!" He is our leader, but more than that He speaks for Christ in Christ's Church. He does not have to speak ex-cathedra to require our obedience to his teaching on faith and morals.

The great heartbreaker is that those who are no longer "real" Catholics do not leave the Church for other pastures where their theology meshes more with our Protestant brethren. They remain in the Church — not out of love for what the Church represents and teaches, but to weaken it and bring it to its knees until it conforms with their Modernist views — at which time it will be anything but the Holy, Roman, Catholic Church of Jesus Christ and His Mother. But we know the Gates of Hell will NOT prevail against the Church, and the remnant will be protected by Christ for the glorious reign of peace (as prophesied by Pope John Paul II), beginning in the Golden Jubilee Year of 2000.

The first part of this book discussed the nature of the Modernist heresy and gave some suggestions to help us stand against that serious threat within the Church. The following pages are meant to provide some practical suggestions that could help preserve the REMNANT FLOCK. For those who scoff at words like the coming chastisement, Fatima, Akita, Medjugorje, Garabandal and Las Salette, this book will be a waste of their time unless the supernatural action of God's grace works the very miracle in their souls that they deny is even possible. Remember — these misguided souls reject the supernatural. God's mercy, however, can overcome all obstacles and I pray that all of those who have the strong desire to be part of the faithful remnant will pray with all their strength for the grace of conversion for all of us — the misguided and the sinners!

Presented in sequence in the next chapters are some practical actions that can be taken at the parish level, and some clear words from the Bible and Vatican Council II on the responsibility of bishops and priests in preserving the traditional Catholic Faith and how every Catholic family or individual who desires to be responsible and faithful to the Magisterium (authentic teaching authority of the Church), the Holy Father, and the Blessed Mother, can prove their love and loyalty to Jesus Christ Himself. It seems that one heartwarming conclusion can be formed at this time — whosoever tries to successfully be a part of THE REMNANT will also be prepared for THE WARNING and all subsequent happenings that have been prophesied for these end times.

CHAPTER TWO
Faith-Alert at the Parish Level

Congratulate yourself if you currently have a pastor who is orthodox in his faith, loyal to the Pope and his encyclicals, gives a homily based on the readings and the Gospel of the Mass, doesn't deviate from the approved rubrics and is scrupulously complying with only the authorized wording of the Consecration. Treasure him and fight to keep him in your parish. The odds are his replacement will not fulfill these qualifications.

His personality and human quirks and failings, idiosyncrasies, and human faults, and even obvious personal sins are not a serious impediment to the salvation of the soul of the parishioner. That rare priest with the perfect disposition and loving touch cannot be hoped for but once in a great while. With an aging priesthood and a shortage of young priests exiting the seminaries, we can count on seeing more and more ailing priests who will be limited in their workload capacity. We should be grateful if the pastor and his associate pastors are providing solid Catholic teaching and offering valid Masses. We are not going to have these kinds very long and it is prophesied that we will need to "go underground" to worship at a valid Mass with a loyal priest in the not-too-distant future.

Not only should we participate in the Mass with our full attention and a sincere heart wanting to please the Lord and hear the magnificent contents of the word, but we *need* to in order to listen critically — listening to learn and evaluate. If one hears anything questionable or strange that doesn't conform to our traditional Faith, make a mental note of it. The most recently approved *Catechism of the Catholic Church* is a perfect reference book with which a serious Catholic should be very familiar. When something said contradicts the Gospel or what you have always known and believed to be Catholic teaching, very politely ask questions for clarification. Be certain you listen well and don't be confrontational in tone or attitude. You have a very legitimate right to ask for clarification, and it is always possible that you have always had wrong information yourself and may, indeed, need to be shown the correct information. You are not looking for a fight. You want information, cooperation, and peace.

CCD and Sex Education

If you have children enrolled in CCD or in a parochial school sit in on the classes. You have a right to do so. Ask the CCD coordinator for this permission and ask the principal for permission. Public schools permit this and here where we are dealing with the souls of our children we have a higher priority to sample classes to insure that only the TRUTH is being taught. Especially in the case where the CCD program or the parochial school program is presenting any kind of sex education program.

There are nightmarish stories about sex education programs that are an abomination. Object to those sex education programs that explain and subtly endorse homosexuality. No discussion on the gay orientation or any aspect of that lifestyle can ever be justified in a Catholic school. Those programs are ostensibly used to help us understand the plight of the lesbian and the homosexual, but they do much more harm than good. Ask yourself this question — would it have been necessary for *you* in CCD or parochial school to have had that kind of instruction to make you a better Catholic or to better understand your Catholic Faith? It's much better to do the teaching at home if you can. For adults? Perhaps! For children? No!

There are other places better suited for presenting that material and the parents should make that determination for themselves. If necessary, the parent should attend some preparation after consulting a Catholic counselor and decide if and when your child needs to hear that "stuff" in elementary or junior high school. Yes, sad to say, there are some Catholic teachers and clergy who will endorse that life-style if given the opportunity. Need we go into the problems of pedophilia and other troubles in some seminaries? *You* are responsible to protect your children.

Satan Worship and Witchcraft

Satan worship and witchcraft are popular topics among some public high schoolers. Many of the young are actually participating. Try to find out if there are any "special classes" after school where some teachers are pushing this stuff off on the students. Ask around if your kids and others are using language that would tip you off that they are involved in the occult. Believe me — this is going on in a big way and the kids need to be protected from it if it's in your area. Witchcraft is said to be practiced by some nuns and superstitious practices involving the occult are spreading like wildfire among the youth. Read Malachi Martin's *Windswept House* to see the practice of Satan worship within the Church, and the power of Modernism in *The Keys of the Blood.* Then pray!

New Age Movement

The New Age cult is spreading like a prairie fire in a high wind. It is definitely in the Church in the United States and has a prominent place among some parishes where the sophisticated are determined to wake the rest of us up to what is "real and important" for the modern church today

If you don't know what the New Age cult fosters among their adherents, you can find good books in a Catholic bookstore. Their main thrust is that we are all gods. Their idea of God is more like a cosmic spirit but it is not our God, the Father, the first person of the Blessed Trinity. Their's is not a personal God. They have a firm belief in reincarnation, and basically it is a general quasi-religion that includes the practice of witchcraft, astrology, and spiritualism (communication with the dead). Many of the members of this New Age "religion" are good people and well-intentioned people. Its leaders, however, are leading them away from the faith that could save their souls, away from the Savior Who died for them.

The integration of the New Age Movement into the Catholic belief system is highly dangerous because, among other reasons, Jesus is not recognized as God and most of the aspects of it are incompatible with Christianity. . There is no belief in knowing God through the knowledge of Jesus. There is no belief in the redemption through Jesus. There is no belief in Heaven or hell. It is so broad and general that it defies description yet it has much appeal to many people who are not believers in any organized Christian religion. Catholics must avoid it and be on the alert for its entrance into parish committees and other organizations within the parish. The New Age Movement has in fact entered into the Catholic Church and considerable discernment will be needed on the part of all of us to stop its further progress.

Prayer Groups and Special Devotions

Do you feel that a prayer life is offered in the parish other than obligatory Mass days? Are various spiritual associations encouraged like the Legion of Mary, Blue Army, various secular orders like Carmelites, Benedictines, Franciscans? Some churches have established Family Prayer Nights with Exposition of the Blessed Sacrament. With families under attack from all quarters special prayers in community are sorely needed.

Parishioners can request the First Nine Fridays devotion and the First Five Saturdays devotion. Prayers to the Divine Mercy can be part of Family Prayer Night. The Rosary can be said after daily Mass. Consecration to the Sacred Heart and the Immaculate Heart should be renewed periodically after the Rosary or Chaplet of Mercy. Monthly Confession is a minimum. Fasting on bread and water or some form of mortification ought to become part of the prayer life of families, for those who can participate without risk to health. One most powerful help is the enthronement of the home to the Sacred Heart of Jesus. This protection is most important!

One of the most encouraging signs is the Eucharistic Adoration on the First Friday of the month. The benefits are great for healing within the parish and it means your pastor believes in the True Presence. Or it ought to mean that. If the Eucharist is the Heart of the Church a very special devotion should be shown the Blessed Sacrament including a quiet and reverential environment in the church, especially when the Blessed Sacrament is exposed . I have frequently seen teen-agers going to Holy Communion while chewing gum on the way to the altar.

Can our non-Catholic friends ever be expected to believe that we worship the True Presence? Take a look at the way most folks enter the church, and if they genuflect at all, try to figure what that cute little dance step is that they're attempting as they fly in one fell swoop from aisle to pew. And why is it that as soon as the priest leaves the altar it seems to be a signal for full voice conversation on any subject as if Our Lord had withdrawn to heaven until the next Mass.

John Leary, the locutionist from Rochester, New York says Our Lord told him on April 19, 1996:

"My people, the Evil One has sown the seeds of division in My Church. He is attacking the very fabric of the Faith in removing the reverence for My Blessed Sacrament. Seeds of dissent are threatening the priest's formation in the seminaries. Teachers are teaching their own agenda instead of basic doctrines of the Holy Fathers. As a result you will see a schism come in My Church where an apostate Pope will split the faithful so that My True Church will lie only in the remnant who follow My Will. Pray much My people since this is when your Mass will go underground and will be hard to find."

On May 27, 1996 a locutionist in Ohio, called by the name Sinner/Saint was told by the Blessed Mother that:

"The Church will now divide and the belief in the presence of My Son Jesus Christ in the Holy Eucharist will cease. **Only the remnant will still acknowledge the True Presence..."**

On January 1, 1993, Our Blessed Mother told Fr. Gobbi:

"The hour of its great trial has above all come for the Church, because it will be shaken by the lack of faith, obscured by apostasy, wounded by betrayal, abandoned by its children, divided by schisms, possessed and dominated by Freemasonry, turned into fertile soil from which will spring up the wicked tree of the man of iniquity, the Antichrist who will bring his kingdom into its interior."

Sadie Jaramillo visionary and locutionist, on June 9, 1997 was told by Jesus:

"The blows of God's Almighty Justice will strike as the lightning. It will be swift, mighty, and exact. **The sanctuary of My Church lies in disrepair, turned over to the pastors who are filled with self-indulging design and who do not care for the sheep I have entrusted to them. Is not the true shepherd, vigilant over his flock, leaving the many in search of the one, suffering from the elements to be with his flock? They know not the value of that little soul that they foolishly overlook! But I... have continued to hold open My arms of Mercy, extended open on the Cross awaiting My pastors, My flock. My Mother weeps for this time to come to humanity...**"

The *Catholic Prophecy Update* (newsletter) published by *Signs and Wonders For Our Times* listed some excellent actions that can be taken to prepare spiritually for difficult times: In addition to monthly Confession, the following suggestions were offered, among others:

Mass, daily if possible: frequent visits to the Blessed Sacrament; daily spiritual reading, including the Bible; hang crucifixes, use holy water, help evangelize friends and family; wear a scapular and a Miraculous Medal; enthrone your home to the Two Hearts; make the Divine Mercy Novena frequently, but especially for Mercy Sunday. In addition, one should reconcile with their enemies and antagonists.

Penitential Prayers at Beginning of Mass Not for Mortal Sin

A nightly examination of conscience should be very helpful followed by Confession if necessary. Remember — The Warning! Dare we not be in the state of grace when the Warning is upon us and God reveals to us the condition of our soul as He knows it? We should be prepared for judgement always and we must be worthy to receive Holy Communion.

The Holy Father in 1983 on June 15, in St. Peter's Square said, "In order to receive into oneself the grace of the Eucharistic food, *certain dispositions of soul are required, in the absence of which the meal risks being changed into a betrayal."* The Holy Father cautions us that **we are not to use the penitential preparation at the beginning of Mass to wash us clean of serious sin, or even to rid us of dipositions that are incompatible with receiving Holy Communion worthily** because a person is opposed to welcoming Christ. The Holy Father said:

> *"This penitential preparation would therefore be insufficient for those who have a mortal sin on their conscience. Recourse to the Sacrament of Reconciliation is therefore necessary in order to approach Eucharistic Communion worthily.* The Church hopes, nevertheless, that even beyond this case of necessity, Christians will have recourse to the sacrament of forgiveness with reasonable frequency in order to foster in themselves ever better dispositions.
>
> "The penitential preparation at the beginning of every celebration must not therefore render the sacrament of forgiveness useless, but it must rather revive in the participants the awareness of an ever greater need for purity, and with that, have them increasingly feel the value of the grace of the sacrament.
>
> *"The Sacrament of Reconciliation is not reserved only for those who commit serious sins. It was instituted for the remission of all sins,* and the grace that flows from it has a special efficacy of purification and support in the effort of amendment and progress. It is an irreplaceable sacrament in Christian life; *it cannot be disregarded or neglected if one wants the seed of divine life to mature in the Christian and produce all the desired fruits."*

We only need to look at the few persons in the Confessional lines and the tremendous numbers attending Holy Communion to see that the words of the Holy Father have fallen on deaf ears and see that those in the Church who do not believe in the Real Presence or the sacramental forgiveness of sins have had

their success in indoctrinating the masses. **For them it is only a meal and a memorial: it is no longer the SACRIFICE of the Mass — It is no longer the Body and Blood of Christ!**

A Message for The Remnant

(If you want to be a member of The Remnant you might find hope in this message concerning the faithful Remnant priests.)

John Leary received the following message from Jesus on May 20, 1995:

"My people, why do I see so much division in My Church? I see the hand of the evil one stirring up errors in My priest sons. I am asking all My faithful to hold on to their precious instruction as received from My apostles. Do not twist My laws and traditions for your own convenience. Be true to your conscience and do not let the false teachers lead you astray. My commands are forever and My laws changeless.

"Being modern does not mean you can do as you please. Live by My instruction in the Scriptures and by My love in your heart and you will not be misled. Again, a person of prayer will be led to follow My ways and stay close to My heart.

"Avoid those who teach heresy and stay true to My faithful remnant led by My Pope, John Paul II."

A Warning for America

To John Leary on May 24, 1995 from Jesus:

"My people of America, how many signs will you need to undertand My visitation? You have witnessed many floods, fires, and other disasters and still you have not reformed your lives. It is as if you do not want to believe there is a connection between your sin and these chastisements. No matter how you evaluate these happenings, they are more than normal. My messages to reform your lives have fallen on many deaf ears and cold hearts. Pray for sinners in earnest to change their lives before My judgement comes and it will be too late. These events are warnings to you of your impending fate. Reform your lives, for My love goes out to you and seeks your return."

Reflection on the preceding message to America

These are mighty words to ponder. Jesus is telling America, the whole nation, not just a select group of a particular religion or some particular race of people, or some unfaithful religious, but all of America — that we are in deep trouble with our God. We are not seeing the signs He sends us nor are we listening to the prophet/ messengers He sends us. We are told to pray seriously for those who will otherwise be lost. We have a great responsibility and will be held accountable for souls if we do not pray for them. We are told very emphatically that the fate of this country is not very encouraging. We are so far away from our Father with our deaf ears and cold hearts. Cold hearts are in cold, spiritually dead bodies and woe to us — this is God's description of America!

And still — He waits for our return and He is prepared to receive us in open arms! He never stops loving us — not even a Godless nation like America. In spite of 30 million abortions, sins against nature, and crimes against the poor and defenseless, He will still accept our repentance and forgive us. What a God we have! How fortunate we are. Are we listening? Are we watching for the signs? Are we changing from a Godless nation to a God-fearing nation? Are we going to change as a nation in time to save ourselves from His retribution and from the fate we are facing because of our obstinacy?

The Final Warning

CHAPTER THREE
The Great Assist for Those of the Remnant

The organization established by the Mother of God, Herself, is one of the very best helps for those who desire to be steadfast in living and defending the Catholic Faith in the face of the coming chastisements and persecutions of the Church, as predicted in the book published by Her organization. Her organization is the Marian Movement of Priests and the book is *To The Priests—Our Lady's Beloved Sons,* now in its 16th edition. The earthly leader of the organization is Fr. Stefano Gobbi to whom Mary reveals Her messages concerning these end times and the coming persecution of the Church. Her organization for priests is also open to membership of the religious and laity.

Please, dear reader, do not become impatient with the thought of having yet one more book to fit into your reading schedule. If you are serious about being prepared for the WARNING and the soon to worsen difficulties already facing a loyal Catholic and you seriously desire to be one of THE REMNANT, you *should* obtain a copy of this book. I believe that with a copy of the Holy Bible, a copy of the authorized *Catechism of the Catholic Church,* and a copy of *To The Priests* you will be well prepared for what the immediate future brings, and you will have the ammunition you need to defend your Faith against all heresies and those foisting them onto the Church and its unsuspecting members.

Father Joseph Hebert, S. M. Supports The Marian Movement of Priests (MMP)

Since 1973, Fr. Stefano Gobbi has been receiving locutions (messages) from the Blessed Mother. The messages now fill the 16th edition up through the year 1996 and have contained numerous prophecies concerning the difficult times ahead for the Church and her loyal members. Mary describes Her special cohort, who with Her Immaculate Heart will triumph over Satan and move forward to an era of world peace. But before the Triumph of Her Immaculate Heart tremendous punishments for the world will first take place. Who is the cohort She speaks of? It is made up of the priests, religious and laity who are loyal to Mary, the Magisterium (authentic teaching authority of the Church) and Her Son, along with the angels. Satan will be defeated but only after a schism befalls the Church and a tremendous amount of suffering besets the Holy Father. When does much if not most of this chastisement take place? Mary says by the Golden Jubilee Year of Two Thousand Her Immaculate Heart will have triumphed. What are we to do for protection from the rampant evils that overwhelm the world? We are to take refuge under the mantle of the Blessed Mother, pray and do penance, and seek the help of our guardian angels.

Her book is filled with prophecy for what She Herself calls "the end times," but She takes extra care to point out that the *end times* in no way refers to the end of the world, but rather to an end of an era, after which life on this earth will no longer resemble what we are now familiar with. A glorious time of peace will prevail for a time after She and the angels defeat Satan and his crowd. His crowd includes those who are following or teaching strange errors and heresies and who will not repent of their ways. It includes the laity, nuns, priests and bishops, and cardinals who have betrayed Our Lord and the Church by deserting the traditional doctrines and beliefs of the Roman Catholic Church.

I will now quote extensively from Fr. Hebert's book *The Tears of Mary and Fatima. Why?* (Copyright 1983). Fr. Hebert is a very prominent author and has lectured extensively at numerous Marian Conferences. His Chapter VI discusses the purpose and strength of the MMP and the whole book discusses the reason for Mary's tears in various apparitions and as manifested in certain images of Mary in recent years:

"First, concerning one of the numerous Marian images that wept in Italy in recent years. Mary, on July 13, 1973, thanked Fr. Gobbi for offering Mass before that image of Her: 'How I appreciated the homage you rendered Me this morning! You came to Ravenna to celebrate Mass before My image that sheds tears, wishing to console My Immaculate Heart. How I rejoiced at your intention: so filial, so affectionate, and so delicate! Yes, you truly consoled Me: You changed My tears into smiles, My sorrows into joy. I smiled and blessed you.'"

Mary went on to explain the reason for Her tears, that they were the tears of a Mother weeping over Her children. It was because many of them were forgetful of God, steeped in sins of the flesh and heading for irreparable ruin. She said that many of Her tears would be wasted on a large number of sinners because of their indifference.

What hurt Mary most, She said, was that some of Her priest sons, Her chosen and consecrated ones, contributed most to Her tears because of their lack of love for Her, their not listening to Her Son's promises, their neglect of Him in the Blessed Sacrament and their abandonment of Him in the tabernacle. She welcomed the Marian Movement of Priests and She blessed it.

"On December 1, 1973, Mary spoke to Father Gobbi about the great evil of atheism and of some unbelieving priests, who wore the guise of lambs but who were real wolves within the Church. She spoke of God's justice which would soon break loose against Satan and his camp because of the love, prayers, and sufferings of the elect. If men only knew, Mary said, of the great and inexpressible tribulations in the making, they might be converted.

"Mary complained: 'But who listens to My messages, who has understood the meaning of My tears, of My maternal invitations?' It was due to the few rare and ignored souls who did pay attention here that the chastisement was pushed back. It might be commented here that we learn from various apparitions and private revelations that "the threatened chastisement" has been pushed back again and again because of the reparation made by chosen souls and because of the intervention of Mary.'"

"On October 30, 1975, Mary said, 'My tears are shed in many places to bring them all back (errant priests) to My sorrowful Heart of a Mother. The tears of a Mother succeed in moving even the most hardened hearts. Now, even My tears of blood leave so many of My sons completely indifferent! My messages will multiply all the more when the voices of my ministers refuse to proclaim the Truth.'

"Mary went on to point out important truths that were neglected in preaching: heaven, the Cross that saves, sin that wounds Her Heart and that of Jesus; hell; the need for prayer and penance.

"The comment might be made here that it is obvious to anyone cognizant of certain conditions and happenings in the Church, that there is much cause for the tears of Mary, either personal, spoken of by Her, or vicariously shed through Her many images, even tears of blood. When, we might ask, in all the history of the Church have appeared so many serious, sorrowful and striking signs; 'Signs of the Times!'"

"On January 21, 1978, Mary expressed to Fr. Gobbi such anguish... She was pleading, begging for help from Her priest sons on all sides and backing up Her pleas with reference to various unusual supernatural manifestations. 'I am pleading with you through manifestations that are becoming more numerous and more evident: My tears, My apparitions, My messages... Priests in particular should listen to these salvos of claims as to the authenticity of Mary's mission in the modern world. Further, they have a terrible responsibility where they ignore such numerous obvious signs, and where they do not take the time to protect seers and to foster the cause of genuine messengers of Mary who present authentic signs given to endorse them...'"

Fr. Hebert strongly recommends the reading of *To The Priests* and it is obvious he feels strongly about the way Our Blessed Mother feels about Her priest sons. The laity has a grave responsibility to pray for priests and bishops who are under severe attack from Satan in these end times.

CHAPTER FOUR
The Diocesan Level

The following quotations are selected because of their unique reference to the responsibility of the bishops and the priests in tending to the salvation of their flock, the Church. Please pay particular attention to what St. Peter says and the words from Vatican Council II. The Modernists and liberals in the Church have a very bad habit of quoting Vatican Council II as the authoritative source for the heresy and strange teachings they hold dear. They need to read Vatican Council II documents — perhaps for the first time, to see their responsibility is to adhere to the written and traditional teachings of the Church. Appropriate change?Yes. Heresy? No.

Hebrews 13: 7-9a

Remember your leaders who spoke the word of God to you; consider how their lives ended, and imitate their faith. Jesus Christ is the same yesterday, today, and forever. Do not be carried away by all kinds of strange teaching.

1 Timothy 4:16

Watch yourself and watch your teaching. Persevere at both tasks. By doing so you will bring to salvation yourself and all that hear you.

1 Peter 5: 1-4

To the elders among you I, a fellow elder, a witness of Christ's sufferings and sharer in the glory that is to be revealed, make this appeal. God's flock is in your midst; give it a shepherd's care. Watch over it willingly as God would have you do, not under constraint, and not for shameful profit either, but generously. Be examples to the flock, not lording it over those assigned to you, so that when the chief Shepherd appears, you will win for yourselves the unfading crown of glory.

From the decree on the ministry and life of priests of Second Vatican Council (Presbyterorum ordinis, Cap. 3, 12)

"By the sacrament of Orders priests are formed in the image of Christ the Priest, to be ministers of Christ the Head in constructing and building up His whole Body, the Church, as fellow-workers with the order of bishops.

"In the consecration of baptism they have already received, in common with all Christians, the sign and gift of so great a vocation and grace that, even in their human weakness, they have the power, and the duty, to seek perfection, in accordance with our Lord's words: 'Be perfect, then, as your Father in heaven is also perfect.'

"Priests are obliged in a special way to acquire this perfection. By receiving Holy Orders they have been consecrated in a new way, and made living instruments of Christ the eternal Priest, so as to be able to continue through the years Christ's wonderful work which, by divine power, has restored to wholeness the entire family of man.

"Since each priest acts, as far as he may, in the person of Christ Himself, he is given a special grace to help him grow toward the perfection of the one whose role he plays, as he miniters to his flock and the whole people of God. He receives grace for the healing of human weakness from the holiness of Christ, who became for us a high priest, holy, innocent, undefiled, separated from sinners...

"As they exercise the ministry of the Spirit and of holiness, they are strengthened in the spiritual life, provided that they are docile to Christ's spirit, Who gives them life and is their guide. By the sacred actions they perform daily, and by their entire ministry in communion with their bishop and fellow-priests, they are set on the way to perfection.

"The holiness of priests is itself an important contribution to the fruitfulness of their ministry. It is true that God's grace can effect the work of salvation even through unworthy ministers, but God ordinarily prefers to show His wonders by means of those who are more submissive to the inspiration of the Holy Spirit, and, who through close union with Christ and holiness of life are able to say with St. Paul: 'I live, but no longer is it I who live, it is Christ who lives within me.'"

From the dogmatic constitution on Divine Revelation of the Second Vatican Council (Dei Verbum, nn. 7-8) (How God's revelation is handed on)

"Christ the Lord, in whom the whole revelation of the most high God is brought to completion, commanded the apostles to preach the Gospel to all mankind. The Gospel, promised through the prophets, was fulfilled in His own person and promulgated by His own lips. The apostles were to proclaim it as the source of all saving truth and all moral discipline, and in so doing to communicate the gifts of God to man.

"This command was faithfully carried out. First, by the apostles, who, *in their preaching by word of mouth, their example and their instructions handed on what they had received from Christ's lips*, from His life among them, and from His actions, or had learnt from the prompting of the Holy Spirit; then by those apostles and apostolic men *who committed the message of salvation to writing, under the inspiration of the same Holy* Spirit... *What was handed on to the apostles comprises all that makes for holy living among God's people and worship of their faith. So, in its teaching, life and worship the Church perpetuates and transmits to every generation all that it is, and all that it believes.*"

From a sermon by Saint Fulgentius of Ruspe, bishop: Who are the stewards, who is the Master? (Certainly not the theologians)

"The Lord, in His desire to explain the special function of those servants whom He placed over His people, said: 'Who do you think is the faithful and wise steward whom his master has set over his household to give them their portion of food at the proper time? That servant is blessed if he is found doing this when his master comes.'

"And who is the master? None other than, Christ who said to His disciples: *'You call me teacher and master, and you are right, for so I am.'* And who is the master's household? Surely, it is the Church which the Lord redeemed from the power of the adversary, and which He purchased for Himself, thereby becoming its master. This household is the holy Catholic Church which is so fruitfully extended far and wide over the world, rejoicing that it has been redeemed by the precious Blood of the Lord. As the Lord Himself says: *'The Son of Man came not to be served but to serve, and to give His life as a ransom for many.'* Furthermore, He is the Good Shepherd Who has laid down His life for His sheep; the Good Shepherd's flock is this household of the Redeemer.

"But who is the steward who must be both faithful and wise? The apostle Paul tells us when he says of himself and his companions: *'This is how one should regard us, as servants of Christ and stewards of the mysteries of God. Morover, it is required of stewards that they be faithful.'*

"But this does not mean that the apostles alone have been appointed our stewards, nor that any of us may give up our duty of spiritual combat, and, as lazy servants, sleep our time away, and be neither faithful or wise. For the Blessed Paul tells us that the bishops too are stewards. *'A bishop,'* he says, *'must be blameless because he is God's steward.'*

"We bishops, then, are the servants of the householder, the stewards of the Master, and we have received the portion of food to dispense to you. If we should wonder what that portion of food is, the blessed apostle Paul tells us when he says: *'To each according to the measure of faith which God has assigned to him.'* Hence, what Christ calls the portion of food, Paul calls the measure of faith. We may therefore take this spiritual food to mean the venerable mystery of the Christian faith. And we give you this portion of food in the Lord's name as often as we, enlightened by the gift of grace, teach you in accordance with the rule of the true faith. In turn, you daily receive the portion of food at the hands of the Lord's stewards when you hear the word of truth from the servants of God"

These readings provided above were selected to indicate from authoritative sources the heavy responsibility of bishops and priests in teaching the faith. Please study all of these readings again, and while doing so, compare the requirement for bishops and priests to preserve the faith as handed from the apostles by word of mouth and writing, with the heresy of Modernism and New Age, deviations from the Bible, especially on the marrying of priests, demands for women-priests, and the status of homosexuals. Compare the old traditional teachings with today on the Confession, Mass, True Presence in the Eucharist, and importance of the Eucharist.

The bishops are the primary stewards of the Catholic Faith, along with the priests. The liberal bishops who are today reinterpreting the traditions of the Faith, ignoring papal encyclicals or distorting them and otherwise no longer presenting the one true Church's teachings are Judases, feigning loyalty to the Magisterium and "Peter," while undermining the Faith. The priests that comply with such bishops' commands are as guilty of betrayal of the Faith and of Jesus Christ as are the bishops they follow.

Some might ask: *What can a priest do when under the thumb of such a renegade bishop?* The answer is not an easy one, but they are responsible to follow their conscience to follow the true teachings of Christ, and do whatever it requires to not participate in heretical teachings and practices, at whatever cost to them career wise or otherwise, or it will cost them their soul and perhaps thousands of others in their flocks.

The Final Warning

Conclusion

It is hoped that reading through this book, perhaps at least twice, the readers will get the insights, knowledge, and inspiration to safeguard the Faith as they have learned it from their parents or other orthodox believers. Perhaps they will qualify to be part of the Remnant Flock of Jesus Christ and His Mother. May the Holy Spirit enlighten all of us!

May the Holy Trinity strengthen us to defend the one, holy, Catholic Faith and thereby become a part of Mary's cohort and thereby save our souls!

The priests are the chosen sons of Jesus and Mary. The problems in the priesthood and the Church can be attributed not only to Satan, but to the Catholic population as a whole because we have never satisfied the demands of the Gospel or Mary to pray and change our ways. Since the warnings at La Salette in 1846 we have been told what will happen if man does not change. In Fatima and for 16 years in Medjugorje we have been asked to change, live the commandments, mortify ourselves, and pray for priests. We now see the fruits of our non-efforts and we have no one to blame but ourselves. But we have a merciful God and He awaits our return. Will we be prepared for the Warning and *what follows*?

The Final Warning

Bibliography

Holy Bible

Conchita. Edited by M. M. Philipon, O. P. 1978.

Christ Denied. Rev. Paul A. Wickens. Tan Pub. , 1982.

Divine Mercy in My Soul. Sr. M. Faustina Kowalska. 1987.

Faith is Greater Than Obedience. Translated by Elizabeth Cattana. 1988.

Keys of the Blood. Dr. Malachi Martin.

Light of Love. Patricia Devlin. Queenship Publishing, 1995.

Liturgy of the Hours (Divine Office).

Message of the Lady of All Nations, The. Edited by Josef Kunzli. 1996.

Our Lady of Light. Chanoine C. Barthas & Pere G. da Fonseca, S. J. 1947.

Please Come Back to Me and My Son. Christina Gallagher. 1992.

Personal Revelations of Our Lady of Light. Edited by Gerald G. Ross. 1992.

Prepare for the Great Tribulation and the Era of Peace. John Leary. Queenship Publishing.

The Tears of Mary and Fatima — Why? Fr. Albert J. Hebert.

To The Priests—Our Lady's Beloved Sons. Fr. Stefano Gobbi.

Windswept House. Dr. Malachi Martin.

The Final Warning

Declarations

Since the abolition of Canon 1399 and 2318 of the former Canonical Code by Pope Paul VI in *AAS 58 (1966) 1186*, publications about new appearances, revelations, prophecies, miracles, locutions, etc. , have been allowed to be distributed and read by the faithful without express permission of the Church, providing that they contain nothing which contravenes faith and morals. Therefore, no *Imprimatur* is necessary.

In *Lumen Gentium,* Vatican II, Chapter 12 reads, "Such gifts of grace, whether they are of special enlightenment or whether they are spread more simply and generally, must be accepted with gratefulness and consolation, as they are specially suited to, and useful for, the needs of the Church... Judgements as to their genuineness and their correct use lies with those who lead the Church and those whose special task is not to extinguish the spirit but to examine everything and keep that which is good..."

"Extinguish not the spirit. Despise not prophecies. But prove all things; hold fast to that which is good." (1 Thess. 5, 19-21)

"In cases like this [apparitions], it is better to believe than not to believe, for, if you believe, and it is proven true, you will be happy that you have believed, because our Holy Mother asked it. If you believe and it is proven false, you will receive all blessings as if it had been true, because you believed it to be true."

— His Holiness, Urban VIII (Pope, 1623-1644)

The Final Warning

Acknowledgements

I first want to express my pleasure in being associated, as an author, with Queenship Publishers, because of the effort this company has made to publish traditional Catholic material for the public. To Fr. Marcos Velasquez for his review of part of the manuscript, his helpful suggestions, and his personal example as a loyal Catholic priest, I say thanks. To the members of The Remnants of the Two Sacred Hearts prayer group in Tucson, Arizona for their prayers for my wife Lucy and me, I say God Bless You. To Fr. Antonio Ruiz whose homily on Fatima inspired me to press on with this book, thanks!

Paul A. Mihalik, Sr.

About the Author

Paul A Mihalik, Sr. is a member of the Secular Order of Discalced Carmelites. He possesses three Masters Degrees; has been a teacher, adjunct university professor for Embry-Riddle Aeronautical University, a school administrator, and marriage and family counselor. He retired as a Lt. Colonel from the United States Air Force in 1968. Originally from Pittsburgh, Pennsylvania, he has lived in Arizona since 1966. He is married to Lucy for 47 years and they have seven children. He and Lucy have dedicated themselves to serving the Church in whatever way they are called to do so. He is the author of *How To Start a Lay Carmelite Community* (Carmelite Press), 1990; *Patagonia Profile* (1985); and *Our Lady of The Sierras,* 1994, a booklet on the Cross Project in Hereford, Arizona. He lectures on the American Civil War, the Custer years, and religion, and has produced an amateur creation on video-tape of the life of St. Therese of Lisieux with the permission of The Lisieux Carmel in France. Much of his time is now spent in lecturing on the messages of the Blessed Virgin Mary from La Salette to the present and conducting days of recollection with Lucy in Tucson, Arizona. He is available to give presentations in state and out of state. Phone (520) 394-2018 in Patagonia, Arizona.